101 SECRETS

of

"CANADIAN

CULTURE"

WORKBOOK

for TEACHERS

by Catherine (Kate) Maven

First Printing: 2019

ISBN: 978-1-9992486-5-9
Otter-Girl Press
Burlington, Ontario, Canada
https://sleepingcat.wixsite.com/ottergirlpress

With love and gratitude

to all of my ESL colleagues

who ~~bugged~~ *encouraged* me

to write this book.

Thanks for your

support &

feedback!

Contents

This workbook is a companion to my book, "100 Secrets of Canadian Culture" (available on Amazon in most regions). I wrote the book because, with a lifetime of experience in Canada as an educator, a mother of three, and as a worker in banking, computers, marketing and employment counselling, I have discovered that a lot of the social rules in Canada aren't clearly explained anywhere.

As a teacher of English as a Second Language for more than thirty years, I have shared most of these "secrets" with my newcomer ESL students, who have told me that this information really helped them to integrate into Canada. Actually, it was at their request that I wrote the book. – And once I had shared the "100 Secrets" book with my colleagues, they asked me to write this workbook!

Here are my 101 WORKSHEETS – one for each "secret" – to use with your class. There are a variety of activities included, such as conversation questions, brainstorming worksheets, surveys and writing exercises.

ANSWERS (where they may be helpful) are at the back of the book. Please keep in mind that, while I've tried to research as many statistics as possible to support my opinions, these are my opinions. If you have had different experiences in Canada, please share them with your students. I tell my students there is no single "Canadian culture". I hope this book provides opportunities for discussion and discovery!

I've included some topics to Google, too, if you want further information about some of the topics in this book.

WARMUP: WHAT DO YOU ALREADY KNOW ABOUT CANADA? – QUIZ

Answer the following questions *TRUE* or *FALSE* to find out just how much of a 'Canuck' you already are!

1. 75% of Canadians speak English as their mother tongue   _____

2. Chinese (Mandarin) is the 3rd most common language in Canada   _____

3. Canadians don't say, "How are you?" every time they meet   _____

4. You should stand an arm's length away from a Canadian when you talk   _____

5. Canadians are very emotional in public   _____

6. Canadians are reserved with strangers, but friendly if you get to know them   _____

7. Canadians usually initiate friendships with their new neighbours   _____

8. If you're invited to dinner, you can always bring your kids   _____

9. You should BYOB (Bring Your Own Beverage) to a party   _____

10. Canadians usually live together before they get married   _____

11. Men and women share housework equally   _____

12. The parents of the bride usually pay for the wedding   _____

13. After a divorce, most Canadians share custody of the kids   _____

14. Employers in Canada consider volunteer work almost equal to paid work   _____

15. All Canadians earn equal pay for equal work   _____

16. Being late for work can get you fired   _____

17. Canadians socialize with their boss   _____

18. A handshake contract is legal in Canada   _____

19. The police in Canada are mostly honest   _____

20. Kids can stay home alone after 12 years old   _____

21. Canadians are indirect when delivering bad news   _____

22. Canada doesn't have social classes   _____

Answers on pg. 117

SECRET #1: MULTICULTURALISM – EXPLORING CULTURAL PRECONCEPTIONS

Work with partners from 2-3 other countries. Try to GUESS the ANSWERS about your partners' cultures. After everyone has guessed, share the results and see if you were right!

NAME:	PARTNER #1:	PARTNER #2:	PARTNER #3:
CHALLENGE:	COUNTRY:	COUNTRY:	COUNTRY:
1. Name 3 things that are usually on the table for each meal.			
2. Name 2 traditions connected to getting married.			
3. What do co-workers say to each other every day?			
4. At what age do children usually begin to live independently?			
5. How late will guests stay at a party?			
6. What should you take if you are invited to dinner?			
7. How spicy is most of their cuisine? (mild, medium, spicy)			
8. Name 3 things you shouldn't do in public.			

SECRET #2: COURTESY – EVERYDAY RESPONSES

WHEN SOMEONE SAYS …	WHAT SHOULD YOU SAY?
Why did you come to Canada?	
Can I bring a friend to your party?	
I just graduated from university.	
How much do I owe you for dinner?	
My son Timmy's in trouble at school again.	
Would you like a diet Coke?	
They didn't hire me.	
What's Rick's last name?	
Will you lend me $1,000,000?	
Can I borrow some paper?	
I'll buy the drinks.	
May I use your phone?	
Did you pass the test?	
I hope I get the job.	
Can I date your sister?	
I think we should call off the meeting.	
Can I come too?	

Answers on pg. 118

SECRET #3: SMILE! – CONVERSATION

1. Is it normal to smile a lot in your country of birth? Why or why not?

2. Do children smile more than adults in your country of birth?

3. Do seniors smile more than younger adults in your country of birth?

4. Do women smile more than men in your country of birth?

5. Would you smile more at home, at work, or at a friend's place?

6. Why do you think Canadians smile at each other as much as they do?

7. Do you think Canadians' smiles are genuine, or "plastic"?

8. Do you tend to trust someone who smiles at you, or someone who appears to be more serious?

9. Why do you think Canadians tend to focus on the positive things, and ignore or deny uncomfortable feelings and situations?

10. Is a "positive attitude" important in your culture? What about at work?

11. Which professions are more likely to smile?

12. People say, "You can smile with your mouth, but with a real smile, you also smile with your eyes."

SECRET #4: DIVERSITY – FIND SOMEONE WHO ...

FIND at least 1 person in your class for whom the description is TRUE. (Write as MANY names as you can in each box!)

Name(s):				
Is an aunt	Is on a diet	Is a non-smoker	Plays a musical instrument	Attends a place of worship regularly
Has recently eaten at an "ethnic" restaurant	Lives with relatives	Does volunteer work	Has lived on a farm	Thinks cold pizza is great for breakfast
Is a vegetarian	Has three or more siblings	**One surprising thing about *ME***	Has been to another province in the last 6 months	Is a member of a cultural organization
Has had 2 or more careers	Has visited 3 or more countries	Knows what Kwanza is	Has lived in 2 or more countries	Knows what Hanukah is
Has worked at a place where uniforms are required	Speaks more than two languages	Is an uncle	Has parents living in another country	Is an only child

SECRET #5: GENDER IDENTITY – SELF-REFLECTION

Answer the following questions to the best of your ability:

1. When's the first time you can remember learning that some people are lesbian, gay, bisexual or queer?

2. Where did most of the influence of your initial impressions/understanding of lesbian, gay, bisexual and queer people come from? (e.g., family, friends, television, books, news, church)

3. When's the first time you can remember learning that some people are transgender?

4. Do you think the number of transgendered people is increasing, or only our awareness and acceptance of them?

5. Where did most of the influence of your initial impressions/understanding of transgender people come from? (e.g., family, friends, television, books, news, church)

6. How have your impressions/understanding of LGBTQ (lesbian, gay, bisexual, transgender, and queer/questioning) people changed or evolved throughout your life?

7. Have you ever met anyone who is LGBTQ?

8. How might you react if you found out your child or grandchild was LGBTQ?

9. If your child or grandchild was LGBTQ, how would you want them treated by other people?

Questions adapted from: **https://thesafezoneproject.com/activities/**
(Used with permission)

SECRET #6: WE DON'T SAY "HELLO" & "GOODBYE" – GREETINGS – BRAINSTORMING

How could you START & END a conversation …

... at School?	

... on the Telephone?	

... in a Public Place?	

... at Work?	

SECRET #7: DON'T ALWAYS ASK, "HOW ARE YOU?" – GREETINGS – CONVERSATION

Conversation Questions About PHYSICAL CONTACT in your COUNTRY OF BIRTH:

- How do people in your country of birth usually greet each other at work/school?

- How do people in your country of birth usually greet each other at home?

- Are greetings different between 2 women, 2 men, or men & women? How?

- Who is it okay for you to touch socially? (strangers, friends, family, etc.)

- Who isn't it okay for you to touch?

- Are people usually physically affectionate to their children out in public? (hugging and/or kissing)

- Are people physically affectionate to their children at home?

- Is it okay to show physical affection to other people's children without the parent's permission?

- Are people usually physically affectionate to their spouse / love partner out in public? (hugging and/or kissing)

- Are people usually physically affectionate to their spouse / love partner at home?

- Do you use "love names" for family members / spouses?

- e.g., honey, darling, dear, etc.

- Do women hold hands with female friends while walking or talking?

- Do men hold hands with male friends while walking or talking?

- Is there an age limit on these activities (childhood, adult, seniors)?

- How do people usually say "Goodbye" in your country of birth? Is there a physical action included?

SECRET #8: PRACTICE MAKING SMALL TALK – CONVERSATION

Go around the classroom. Speak to each of your classmates. Have SHORT conversations to practice using and responding to some of the following conversation OPENERS:

Weather

- Nice day, isn't it?
- How is it out there?
- Getting warmer, eh?
- Enjoying the spring?

Comment on something you see

- Beautiful picture... Who painted it? / **Photo:** Where was it taken?
- What a cute dog! What breed is he? Or is it a she?
- What a cute baby! Is it a he or she? How old is he/she?

Plans

- Any plans for the weekend?
- Where are you off to on you next trip?
- Any plans for the holidays?

Compliments

- New jacket? I like the style. Where did you get it?
- Did you get a haircut? That new style suits you so well!

Common acquaintances

- How is _____ (our former teacher) these days?
- Tell your mom I said hello. How is she these days?

Other Good Conversation Starters

- Excuse me, is this seat taken?
- Mind if I put my books here?
- I see you're looking at / reading about / watching… (a soccer player....)
- Do you know how to open / shut / adjust / fix this ...
- Do you know where the nearest bank / gas station / grocery store is?

Bad Conversation Openers

- Tell me, where do you live?
- What religion are you?
- I hate the Toronto Maple Leafs, don't you?

SECRET #9: TABOOS – SAFE & DANGEROUS QUESTIONS – SURVEY
RATE the following questions from NOT Taboo (0) to VERY Taboo (5)

QUESTION	YOUR COUNTRY OF BIRTH	IN CANADA
"Do you buy lottery tickets?"		
"Do you drink alcohol?"		
"Do you like to gamble?"		
"Do you have any allergies?"		
"Do you have any illnesses?"		
"Do you have any painkillers with you?"		
"Do you cheat on your spouse?"		
"Do you see fortune tellers?"		
"Do you wear glasses?"		
"Do you wear pajamas to sleep?"		
"What do you think of abortion?"		
"What do you think about euthanasia?"		
"How do you feel about your mother-in-law?"		
"How long do you spend exercising every week?"		
"How many pairs of shoes do you have?"		
"How much do you weigh?"		
"How much money do you earn?"		
"How much money do you spend on going out?"		
"How often do you get drunk?"		
"How often do you take a bath or shower?"		
"How often do you tidy up your house or apartment?"		
"What do you think about nuclear power?"		
"Where do you buy underwear?"		
"Where do you come from?"		
"Where do you usually go on holiday?"		

Answers on pg. 120

SECRET #10: BE CAREFUL WITH PERSONAL QUESTIONS

Use an EMBEDDED QUESTION to "ask permission to ask" these questions:

Information Questions: "Excuse me …	Beginning of noun clause "Excuse me …	Question Word	Subject	Verb
Where is the post office?	Could you please tell me	where	the post office	is?
When is the next bus coming?	Do you happen to know	when	the next bus	is coming?
Who is that man over there?	Do you know	who	that man over there	is?
How much does this _____ cost?	Can you please tell me	how much	this _____	costs?
Where is Claire?				
How old are you?				
Where is the washroom?				
Why did _____ go home?				
When is the summer break?				
Who is the manager or owner?				
What time is it?				
When will you be finished?				
Where will you be tomorrow?				
What do you want?				
How much did you pay for your house?				

Answers on pg. 121

SECRET #11: TONE & BODY LANGUAGE – EXPRESSING EMOTIONS

Write down which EMOTION (anger, joy, humour, reluctance, excitement, sadness, confusion, flirtation, interest, anxiety, pain, etc.) you think each statement shows. Then PRACTICE using your VOICE to show this emotion!

1. Boy, you're something, do you know that? You are really something! _____

2. Oh, man. I don't want to do this – I really don't. _____

3. I can't believe it! It was the most exciting thing that's ever happened! _____

4. It was so funny! You had to be there – it was a classic! _____

5. Oh, I wish I could go. I'd give anything if I could be there. _____

6. I don't want to talk about it. In fact, I don't even want to think about it. _____

7. I really like you. You're easy to talk to, you know? _____

8. Look, it's none of your business. Okay? Just leave me alone. _____

9. I wish that things were like they used to be. It was a lot easier back then. _____

10. What did you do that for? What's wrong with you? _____

11. God! / Gosh! I'm so nervous. I just can't seem to calm down. _____

12. / Gosh! / Oh God! It hurts! Can't you do something about it? _____

13. I don't care. I really don't care at this point. _____

14. Something's wrong, isn't it? You're afraid to tell me, is that it? _____

15. Did you really? Go on – you're kidding me! _____

16. I'm not sure I understand. Tell me again; I'm just not sure what you mean. _____

17. Where have you been? Do you know how long I've been waiting for you? _____

18. I hope they're all right. I just hope nothing's happened. _____

19. Hey, everything's great! Things couldn't be better: _____

20. Well . . . I mean . . . Okay. Okay. Let me start again. _____

Suggestions for TONE on pg. 122

PHOTOCOPIABLE BY PURCHASING TEACHER

SECRET #12: PERSONAL SPACE – INTERACTIVE ACTIVITY

Instructions for the teacher / facilitator. This is a physical activity which the instructor and the students all experience together. I have used it successfully many times!

1. If you can, section off a portion of your classroom or working space into an area that will fit all of your students with a fair amount of extra room. I move the tables in my class until they form a square.

2. Invite all of the students into the 'enclosed' space. (If anyone is uncomfortable with this exercise, they can remain on the outside of the square, but within arm's reach of the nearest student.)

3. Ask the students to stand – as close as they are comfortable standing – to the nearest person. (Don't say anything yet about men vs. women.)

4. If anyone moves closer to you than arm's length, hold your arm out straight from your shoulder, with your hand up, and tell everyone, "Please don't stand any closer to me than this."

5. Tell the students that if anyone is standing too close to them, it's okay to step back until they feel comfortable, or to politely ask the person to step back.

6. Once everyone has stopped moving, it's time to debrief:

QUESTIONS:

1. What do you notice about our perceptions of personal space?

2. Which culture or individual seems to require the least distance between individuals?

3. Which culture or individual seems to require the most distance between individuals?

4. *Is our comfort zone different for people of the same gender?*

- Ask the students to stand as close as they are comfortable standing to someone of the *same* gender. Remind them it's okay to step away from a person who's standing too close. For students who moved, ask: "Why did you move?"

- Ask the students to stand close as they are comfortable standing to someone of the *opposite* gender. For students who moved, ask: "Why did you move?"

5. Ask the students to help you arrange the classroom back to the normal configuration, and then elicit feedback on how different our cultural and personal requirements are for personal space. Reiterate that it's okay to step back from someone who is standing too close to you.

SECRET #13: AVOID RUDE BODY NOISES & GESTURES – BINGO

This is an activity to practice understanding gestures in Canada.

	B	I	N	G	O
B	Me?	No	Yes	Look at that!	Crazy
I	Shame on you	I feel emotional	I can't hear you	No WAY!	Stop!
N	Calm down	So-so	Good idea	Bad idea	Yesterday / In the past
G	I'm cold	I'm hot	Come here	Go away	I don't know
O	Good luck	Just a minute	I'm thinking	I won't say a word	He's / She's hot! (sexy)

PHOTOCOPIABLE BY PURCHASING TEACHER

GESTURES BINGO – WORDS TO CUT UP FOR CALLING:

(Suggestion: A student who gets BINGO can take a turn doing the gestures.)

Me?	No	Yes	*Look at* that	Crazy
Shame on you	I feel emotional	I can't hear you	No WAY!	Stop!
Calm down	So-so	Good idea	Bad idea	Yesterday / In the past
I'm cold	I'm hot	Come here	Go away	I don't know
Good luck	Just a minute	I'm thinking	I won't say a word	He's / She's hot! (sexy)

GESTURES BINGO – HOW TO ACT OUT THE GESTURES:

1. Me?   = pointing at yourself with raised eyebrows
2. No   = shaking your head
3. Yes   = nodding your head
4. Look at that = pointing – arm out, hand out, palm up (NOT pointing a finger!)
5. Crazy = making circles with a finger beside your temple
6. Shame on you = wagging a finger & frowning (often playful)
7. I feel emotional (women only) = hands palms facing down, fingers toward your face, fingers open, waving like a fan
8. I can't hear you = hand cupped beside your ear
9. No WAY!   = hands open, palms down, gesture from centre to either side
10. Stop!   = arm straight in front of you, palm up (like the police)
11. Calm down   = palms down, fingers open, waving gently away from you
12. So-so   = one hand, palm down, waggling
13. Good idea   = one thumb up
14. Bad idea   = one thumb down
15. Yesterday / in the past = closed fist, thumb extended, point over your shoulder.
16. I'm cold   = shivering, arms crossed, rubbing opposite upper arms
17. I'm hot   = fanning yourself with your hand; wiping imaginary sweat off of your forehead
18. Come here   = whole hand palm up, fingers waving toward your body
19. Go away   = hand, palm down, waving strongly away from you
20. I don't know = one or both shoulders shrugging, hands open in front of you at waist height, palms up (conveys sincerity)
21. Good luck   = index and middle finger crossed
22. Just a minute = index finger held up in front of you
23. I'm thinking = index finger on temple or jaw
24. I won't say a word = pretending to zip your lips closed
25. He/She's hot! (sexy) = hand in front of you, fingers open, shake the hand up & down

---

SECRET #14: PUBLIC DISPLAYS OF EMOTIONS – SURVEY

ANSWER "YES" or "NO" to the following questions, FIRST about your COUNTRY OF BIRTH and then what you know (or think) about CANADIANS:

QUESTION	YOUR COUNTRY OF BIRTH	IN CANADA
1. Is it okay to cry in public?		
2. Is it okay to cry in front of your family?		
3. Is it okay to yell at members of your family?		
4. Is it okay to yell at your spouse?		
5. Is it okay to yell at your child?		
6. Is it okay to yell at your parent(s)?		
7. Is it okay to yell at a neighbour?		
8. Is it okay to yell at a person at work?		
9. Is it okay to yell at someone on the street?		
10. Is it okay to yell at a server in a restaurant?		
11. Is it okay to argue loudly in a restaurant? (debating)		
12. Is it okay to argue loudly at work? (debating)		
13. Is it okay to argue loudly at a friend's? (debating)		
14. Is it okay to argue loudly on the bus? (debating)		
15. Is it okay to argue loudly at home? (debating)		
16. Is there a difference in these rules between men and women?		
a. Who can cry? (men and/or women / children – up to what age?)		
b. Who can yell? (men and/or women)		
c. Who can argue loudly? (men and/or women)		
17. Is there a difference between social classes?		

Answers on pg. 123

SECRET #15: RESTAURANT ETIQUETTE – PRACTICING POLITENESS

Read the following dialogue that takes place in a restaurant. Replace the underlined with MORE POLITE TERMS.

HOST: "Welcome to Chez Nous. This will be your table. Your server will be right with you.

CUSTOMER: "I <u>hate</u> this table! I <u>am not going to</u> sit by the kitchen!"
           1   2

HOST: "I'm sorry, sir. Follow me, and I'll take you to a different one."

CUSTOMER: "<u>I should hope so!</u>"
           3

HOST: "Is this table acceptable?"

CUSTOMER: "<u>I guess it will have to do. Where's my server? I need a drink!</u>"
                                   4

HOST: "Your server will be right with you. His name is Gaston."

SERVER: "Good evening. My name is Gaston. I'll be your server for tonight."

CUSTOMER: "<u>About time!</u> <u>What kind of name is Gaston, anyway?</u>"
           5   6

SERVER: "It's a French name. I'm originally from France."

CUSTOMER: "<u>Whatever. Just get me a whisky sour, STAT. I'm dying here.</u>"
           7   8

SERVER: "Of course, sir. Right away." (Brings the drink and the Menu)

CUSTOMER: "<u>Okay.</u>" (Looks at the menu.) "<u>What won't kill me</u>?"
                                      9

SERVER: "Our Plat du Jour is filet mignon with grilled asparagus, for $39.99"

CUSTOMER: "Well, <u>I guess I'll have that</u>."
                      10

SERVER: "How would you like your steak, sir?"

CUSTOMER: "Rare. I <u>want to hear it Moo when I slice it.</u>"
                             11

SERVER: "Very good, sir. Would you like another whiskey while you wait?"

Answers on pg. 124

SECRET #16: SEPARATE CHECKS IN RESTAURANTS – SURVEY – Who PAYS?

Work with partners from 2 other countries. Try to GUESS the ANSWERS about your partners' cultures. After everyone has guessed, share the results and see if you were right!

	ME	PARTNER'S Name:	PARTNER'S Name:
CHALLENGE:	My COUNTRY:	COUNTRY:	COUNTRY:
1. If 3 friends go out, who pays?			
2. If parents & adult children go out, who pays?			
3. Who pays on a date?			
4. Do you ever split the check?			
5. If it's your birthday, who pays?			
6. Do you pay in cash or with a card?			
7. Do you ever get separate checks?			
8. If 2 siblings go out, who pays?			

SECRET #17: TIPPING – BRAINSTORMING – LET'S DO SOME MATH!

Working with a partner, calculate the approximate tip for the following totals. (Try NOT to use the calculator on your phone unless you have to!)

SITUATION	TOTAL	APPROPRIATE TIP in CANADA
1. Family Restaurant	$50	
2. Expensive Restaurant	$400	
3. Bar	$8	
4. MacDonald's	$18	
5. Tim Hortons	$2	
6. Food Delivery	$30	
7. Haircut (women)	$40	
8. Haircut (men)	$20	
9. Taxi ride	$17	
10. Room Service	$110	
EXAMPLES FROM YOUR COUNTRY OF BIRTH	**AVERAGE TOTAL**	**TIP?**
11. Restaurant		
12. Bar		
13. Coffee Shop		
14. Haircut		
15. Taxi		

Answers on pg. 125

SECRET #18: YOU SHOULD INITIATE FRIENDSHIPS – BRAINSTORMING

In your group, discuss HOW you learned to make friends.

1. Think about when and where or how you met some of your 3-4 closest friends (You can include family members if you want).

2. Who initiated the friendship? (You, or the other person?)

3. How did it start? Tell your group about one of the friendships.

4. As each group member tells his/her story, ask them some questions about this friend, such as:

5. How long have you known him/her?

6. How often do you speak to each other now?

7. How often do you get together?

8. Who initiates the contact? Who does the inviting?

9. When you moved to a new place in the past, did your neighbours do anything special to welcome you? If so, what was it?

10. When someone new has moved in close to you, do you do anything special to welcome them? If so, what?

11. Do you think it's easier for some people to make friends than others? What kind of person makes friends right away?

12. Do we usually have "friendships of convenience" (People we work or go to school with, or live near)?

13. Do you think Canadians are more friendly or less friendly than people in your country of birth, and why?

14. What can you do to overcome your shyness about approaching a new friend here?

SECRET #19: KIDS SHOULD SKATE & SWIM – DO YOUR KIDS DO SPORTS?

CONVERSATION QUESTIONS About Your COUNTRY OF BIRTH:

1. Name 2 common sports that children play.

2. At what age to children start doing sports?

3. Do all children do physical fitness activities in school?

4. At what age does this start and stop?

5. Is it common for children today to learn to swim?

6. Do you know how to swim?

7. Is it too late for you to learn?

8. Where is the nearest pool?

9. Do children learn to skate?

10. Do children socialize by swimming together?

11. Do children socialize by skating together?

12. If not, what sport might they do together for fun?

13. Where would a child do a sport? (Playground, park, arena, etc.)

14. Do you think it's important for children to play team sports?

15. Why do you think skating and swimming are so popular in Canada?

SECRET #20: (MOSTLY) MEN'S SMALLTALK – NAME THE HOCKEY POSITIONS:

– THIS IS <u>OUR</u> TEAM'S END

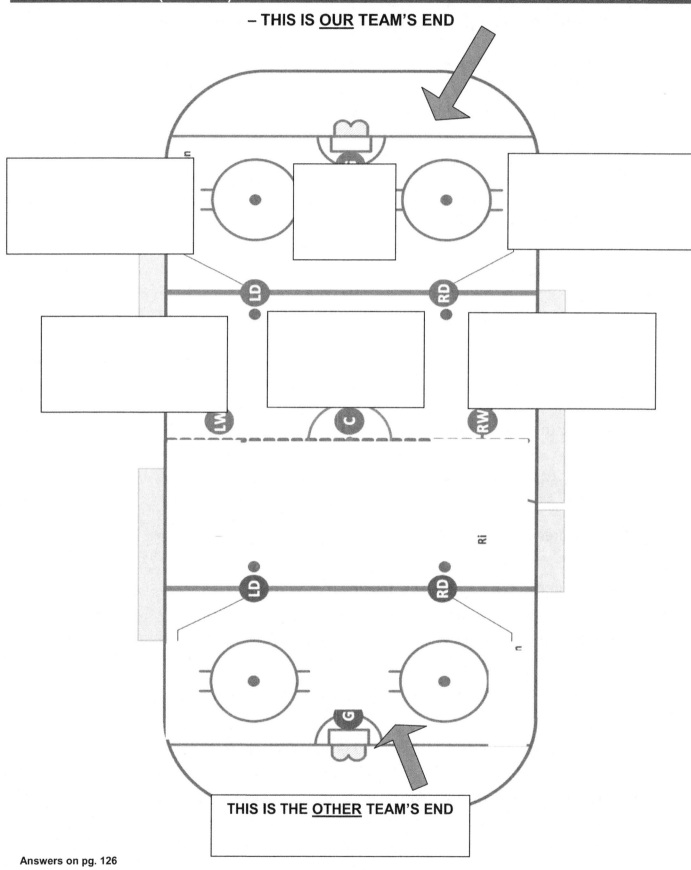

THIS IS THE <u>OTHER</u> TEAM'S END

Answers on pg. 126

SECRET #21: WHERE TO FIND NEW FRIENDS – INTERNET RESEARCH

As a CLASS, BRAINSTORM 8 places where you would typically find a new friend. Divide into teams of 2-3. Each team will search for the address of ONE place to find friends in your town. When you're done, share your information with the rest of the class.

TYPICAL PLACE TO FIND A NEW FRIEND	ADDRESS of a place like this in our town. (Also provide contact phone number, dates & times & any costs, if possible.)
1.	
2.	
3.	
4.	
5.	
6.	
7.	
8.	

SECRET #22: GETTING STARTED WITH A FRIEND – CONVERSATION

CONVERSATION is like TENNIS: a good TIP about keeping a conversation going is to remember, whatever they ask you, answer, and then add, "And YOU?" or "How about YOU?"

Here are some questions to help you get started with a new friend (Remember; only ASK about things YOU want to talk about!):

- What do you like to do in your free time?

- Do you have any hobbies?

    o How long have you been doing them?

    o How did you get started?

- What kind of food / music / books / movies / TV shows do you like?

- What's the last movie you saw?

- Can you recommend a good TV show?

- Are there any books you would really recommend I read?

- Do you know any great YouTubes I should see?

- Are there any comedians you really like?

- What good restaurants do you know of around here?

SECRET #23: DON'T BE A COMPLAINER – REFRAMING JUDGEMENTS

This is a 2-step activity. FIRST, come up with a list of 10 common complaints. Then BRAINSTORM together to come up with another way of stating the same information as a FACT rather than a COMPLAINT. We call this "reframing".

e.g., Talking to your neighbour: "Stop being a jerk." – Reframed: "Please stop putting your garbage in my garbage can. It makes my garbage can too heavy for me to move." ("Jerk" is a JUDGEMENT. Your neighbour's SPECIFIC ACTIONS are FACTS. You show how his actions IMPACT YOU.) There are many excellent websites for learning more about reframing!

COMMON COMPLAINT	REFRAMED as a STATEMENT OF FACT
1.	
2.	
3.	
4.	
5.	
6.	
7.	
8.	
9.	
10.	

SECRET #24: MEETING FOR THE FIRST TIME – ROLE PLAYING

Cut up the cards below and hand them out to your students. Each card represents a Character that we all might meet one day. Have the students take turns being themselves & being these characters to practice "breaking the ice" with these different characters.

"Charlie Co-worker" You work at the same company as your partner but don't do the same job. You don't know much about each other, but have been smiling and saying "Hi" to each other for 6 months. Find out about each other's jobs & families.	**"Nita Neighbour"** You have lived a couple of houses away from your partner for several years. You smile & wave as you get in your cars to take your children to school, but you've never spoken beyond that. Find out what you have in common!
"Simon Supervisor" You used to be the supervisor of your partner when you both worked at the same company, but you have found another job, and now you'd like to become friends. Start by saying something positive about why you'd like to be friends.	**"Shy Sylvia"** You are a VERY shy woman. You have met your conversation partner many times, but you are too shy to speak. Give VERY short answers to his/her questions, and don't ask any questions.
"Chatty Cathy" Your son and your partner's son are best friends, but you don't know each very well. Little does your partner know – you just talk, talk, TALK. Don't let the other person say much. Just keep talking!	**"Community Grandpa"** You are well known in your community as a caring senior. Give your partner some gentle advice about making friends!
"Hostile Henry" You are a co-worker who is a "loner" (prefers to be alone). You have been forced to attend a company party, and your partner is trying to get to know you. Make this Difficult for them!	**"Nancy Know-it-All"** You are an EXPERT on EVERYTHING. Whatever your partner starts talking about, make up some STATISTICS to impress him/her with your SUPERIOR knowledge!
"Nosy Neighbour" You're the nosy neighbour who wants to ask too many personal questions. Keep asking inappropriate questions about your partner's family life.	**"Lonely Les"** You are a VERY lonely neighbour, and you are DESPERATE to make friends. Whatever you partner says, AGREE with him or her. Don't share your own opinions.

SECRET #25: WHO CAN YOU SOCIALIZE WITH AT WORK? – SURVEY

Work with partners from 2 other countries. Try to GUESS the ANSWERS about your partners' cultures. GUESS the right answer for CANADA. After everyone has guessed, share the results and see if you were right!

	PARTNER'S Name:	PARTNER'S Name:	
CHALLENGE:	COUNTRY:	COUNTRY:	COUNTRY: **CANADA**
1. It's normal to socialize with your boss or supervisor after work.			
2. It's okay to chat with co-workers during work hours.			
3. You can socialize with any co-workers after work.			
4. It's common to invite your boss to your house for dinner.			
5. It's important to be friends with the 'RIGHT' people (office POLITICS).			
6. It's normal to use office friendships to advance your career.			
7. It's okay to go out with your colleagues for a drink (alcohol) at lunchtime.			
8. Male and female co-workers can be friends.			

Answers on pg. 127

SECRET #26: MAKING FRIENDS AT WORK – CONVERSATION

Practice making work-related "small talk" with your partners. Try asking some of these questions about your partner's job and family. Since you're pretending to be co-workers, when someone asks you about your job, answer about the job you had in your country of birth (Unless you're working in Canada already!)

PART A: THEIR JOB / CAREER

1. How long have you been with the company?

2. What is the best thing about your job?

3. What's the worst thing?

4. Have you ever had a different career than this one? If so, what was it, and why did you change careers?

5. If you could give me some advice about getting ahead in this career, what would it be?

6. Who or what inspired you to choose this career?

7. Where did you go to school? (How was your school?)

PART B: THEIR FAMILY

8. Do you have family here? – If yes:

   - How old are your kids?

   - Boys or girls?

   - What grade are they in?

   - How do they like their school?

   - Are they taking any lessons? If so, what? Where? Would you recommend it?

9. If NO -

   - Continue with "New Friend" questions (SECRET #24)

SECRET #27: WE TAKE TURNS – PARENTING CONVERSATION

Try to make SMALL GROUPS that contain at least 2 members from the SAME country or region. Discuss the following questions in your group. Find out if there is a cultural element to them, or if it varies more between individuals. Do people from the same region always AGREE?

1. How old are kids when they learn to take turns (in a game, for instance)?

2. Do you remember when you learned to take turns? What happened? (It's okay if you don't remember!)

3. Did you do any special activities to teach your kids (If you have more than one) to take turns?

4. Do you think it's important to be 100% "fair" – that is, should every child get an equal turn? (For example, if one child is younger or smaller when you were playing a sport, did everyone make sure the little one had an equal chance to play?)

5. Is "winning" more important than "being fair"?

6. Do you normally take turns hosting your friends?

7. Do you take turns inviting friends out, or does one person do most of the inviting?

8. Do you take turns paying when you go out with friends? If not, who usually pays, and why?

9. Do you take turns hosting big events with your family? If not, who hosts, and why?

10. Do you think there is anyone who is taking advantage of your generosity?

11. Do you think you are taking advantage of anyone else's generosity?

12. Do you think Canadians REALLY practice "fair turns" or "equal turns"? Why or why not?

SECRET #28: INVITING – ACCEPTING & REFUSING – CONVERSATION

INVITE YOUR PARTNER...	RESPONSE: Please practice ACCEPTING, REFUSING & EXPRESSING UNCERTAINTY
… to come to your house for dinner.	
… to go out with you to a restaurant for dinner (1ST time).	
… to go out with you to a restaurant for dinner (close friend).	
… to go out for coffee (a friend).	
… to go out for coffee (a classmate you don't know very well).	
… to go to a movie with you.	
… to play soccer with you and your friends on Sunday.	
… to go shopping with you and your friends	
… to go on a hike (make sure to tell him/her how far you will walk!)	
… and their spouse to go dancing with you and your spouse.	
… to a party.	
(Your idea.)	

ANSWERS pg. 128

SECRET #29: CAN YOU BRING THE KIDS? ATTITUDES ABOUT OPK (Other People's Kids)

– SURVEY

FIND at least 1 person in your class for whom the description is TRUE. (Write as MANY names as you can in each box!)

Name(s):				
Has only 1 child	Adores kids	Has no kids	Has 1 grandchild	Has 2+ grandkids
Likes to PLAY with kids (What age?)	Likes QUIET kids	Likes NOISY kids	ALWAYS wants friends to bring their kids	Okay for friends to bring their kids SOMETIMES
NEVER wants friends to bring their kids	Has three or more siblings	**MY attitude toward OPK**	Things children should be SEEN and not HEARD	Wants 1 child (someday)
Wants 2+ kids (someday)	Wants 1 child (SOON)	Wants 2+ kids (SOON)	Wants 1+ grandkids (someday)	Wants 1+ grandkids (SOON)
Has worked with kids as a job	Wants to work with kids	NEVER wants to work with kids	Has/had a Nanny	Has been a Nanny

SECRET #30: PUNCTUALITY – SURVEY – HOW IMPORTANT IS IT TO BE ON TIME?

**Work with partners from 2 other countries. Compare your ANSWERS to your partners'.
GUESS the right answer for CANADA.**

HOW IMPORTANT IS IT TO BE ON TIME? RATE the following according to this scale: 0 = not important 1 = a bit important 2 = somewhat important 3 = VERY important				
Type of Appointment	**Scheduled Time**	**PARTNER 1 NAME:**	**PARTNER 2 NAME:**	**CANADA**
Starting Work (hourly work)	9 A.M.			
Starting Work (salaried work)	9 A.M.			
Dentist or Doctor	10:15 A.M.			
Doctor (Specialist)	10:15 A.M.			
School	9 A.M.			
Lunch with a friend at home	12 P.M.			
Lunch with a friend at a restaurant	12 P.M.			
Arriving home for dinner with your family	6 P.M.			
Making dinner for your family (time to finish)	6 P.M.			
A friend's party	8 P.M.			
A work party	8 P.M.			
A performance review	9 A.M.			
A job interview	2 P.M.			

Answers on pg. 129

SECRET #31: WHAT TO BRING? – SURVEY & CONVERSATION ABOUT SOCIALIZING & GIFT GIVING

PART A:

How would you define the differences (in ASSETS)?

	CANADA (GTA) (estimate)	YOUR COUNTRY OF BIRTH:	PARTNER'S COUNTRY OF BIRTH:
ultra wealthy	$ 30 million +		
rich	$10 - $30 million		
well off	$ 5- $10 million		
comfortable	$1 - $5 million		
getting by	$100,000 - $1 million		
struggling	< $100,000		
poor	NO assets		

PART B: Discuss with your group what gifts you would typically give in the following situations. How different is it between wealthy & poor people?

	CANADA	YOUR COUNTRY OF BIRTH:	PARTNER'S COUNTRY OF BIRTH:
dinner hosts (You go to their place for dinner)	- bottle of wine or dessert		
family birthday	- varies		
child birthday (under 12)	- varies ($25?)		
Christmas / New Year's - friend	- varies		
Christmas / New Year's - family	- varies		
housewarming	- houseplant or tree		
engagement	Nothing (a card, maybe)		
wedding	- varies ($200+)		

SECRET #32: BYOB – ALCOHOL CONSUMPTION – CONVERSATION

In your group, discuss some of the following questions regarding alcohol consumption in your country of birth.

1. Are you allowed (legally or religiously) to drink alcohol?

   - If no, do some people drink anyway?

   - Where do they get the <u>booze</u>? (slang word for alcohol)

   - If they get caught, what is the penalty?

2. If you are allowed to drink alcohol, what's the legal drinking age (if any)?

3. At what age do people typically start to drink? (legally or not)

4. Where do you go to drink?

5. Are there places which only sell alcohol, or do they have to serve food, too?

6. Do women and men drink equally?

7. How often do people consume alcohol? (daily, weekly, monthly, etc.)

8. Is drinking alcohol part of the work culture? If so, how?

9. Is drinking alcohol part of the business culture? How?

10. Is there a problem with alcoholism in your country of birth?

   - If so, how big of a problem is it? (Do you know any statistics? Can you Google it?)

   - Is alcoholism equally a problem for men and women?

   - Can children be alcoholics?

   - Are there government-sponsored programs to help people recover from alcoholism?

   - Are there private clinics ("Rehab") to help people recover from alcoholism?

   - Can you prevent alcoholism?

   - Can you 'cure' alcoholism?

SECRET #33: BBQ, GET-TOGETHER OR PARTY? DRESS CODES – SURVEY

Do you have similar dress codes for special occasions in your country of birth? Tell your group what is typical to wear to each of the following occasions:

Dress code & Occasion:	What to wear: Women	What to wear: Men
VERY formal events - some $$$ weddings - galas - state dinners		
Formal events - evening affairs - galas		
Formal, but trendy events - *New trends* for weddings & galas?		
Semi-formal events - between formal and casual. Depends on the time of the event - evening events - concerts - galas		
Festive and fun events - dressy but not formal - garden weddings - summer parties - cocktail parties - New Year's Eve		
Business casual events - casual, but work-appropriate - summer parties - conferences - some weddings & funerals		
Casual events–everyday wear - friends or family gatherings - BBQs, beach party, picnics - casual weddings		

Answers on pg. 130

SECRET #34: HOW LONG IS A GET-TOGETHER? – SURVEY

Work with partners from 2 other countries. Try to GUESS the YES/NO ANSWERS about your partners' cultures & about Canada.

After everyone has guessed, share the results and see if you were right!

	PARTNER'S Name:	PARTNER'S Name:	
CHALLENGE:	COUNTRY:	COUNTRY:	CANADA?
1. It's normal to start a party in the afternoon and continue for 8+ hours.			
2. We will often spend 3-4 hours in a restaurant.			
3. Get-togethers at someone's home usually end about midnight.			
4. It's common for people to sleep over if the party goes late.			
5. Children can stay up as late as they want at a get-together (school night = Sunday-Thursday nights)			
6. Children can stay up as late as they want at a get-together ("weekend night = Fri. & Sat. nights)			
7. You can tell your guests directly that they should go home.			
8. You should **hint** that it's time to go home. (How?)			

Answers on pg. 131

SECRET #35: ARE THEY MARRIED? COMMON-LAW MARRIAGES – CONVERSATION

In small groups, discuss some of the following questions. GUESS whether these are TRUE in CANADA.

1. Are couples allowed to live together without a legal marriage? (Live "common law"?)

   - If yes, has this always been true?

   - When did it start to change?

2. Do partners in common-law relationships have **the following RIGHTS and RESPONSIBILITIES (as legally-married partners would have)?**

   a. Are financially responsible for supporting your biological children (while 'married')?

   b. Are financially responsible for supporting your biological children (after separating)?

   c. Have the same rights to custody & access to children in the case of a breakup?

   d. Have to submit a joint tax return?

   e. Can share health benefits offered through work?

   f. Have the same access to a partner in the hospital?

   g. Have the same right to inherit from their common-law spouse?

   h. Have the same right to 50% of assets in the case of a breakup?

   i. Are financially responsible for their common-law spouse's debts?

   j. Have the same right to spousal support in the case of a breakup?

   k. Have the same right to welfare and disability benefits

   l. Have the same rights regarding immigration sponsorship

   m. Have the same right to make health care decisions for their common-law spouse?

3. Can common-law partners sign an agreement if they want to change some of their rights? (YES – in Canada)

Answers on pg. 132

SECRET #36: HOUSEWORK – EQUALITY BETWEEN MEN & WOMEN? – SURVEY

Let's play a GAME: Look at the following list of 9 countries. Try to rank (from 1 – 9) in which country women do the MOST work (1), to where the BALANCE between men and women is the CLOSEST (9). If your country isn't listed, ADD it & try to GUESS where it would fit in the Ranking. Then guess how many hours each gender spends on housework per day. Finally, add YOUR name and your PARTNERS NAMES and how many hours YOU spend on housework per day. How has this CHANGED over your lifetime?

COUNTRY	RANK: #1 - #9 - In which countries do women do the MOST housework?	How many HOURS per DAY do you think WOMEN spend on housework?	How many HOURS per DAY do you think MEN spend on housework?
Australia			
Canada			
China			
France			
Germany			
India			
Japan			
UK (United Kingdom)			
US (United States)			
YOUR COUNTRY:			
YOUR COUNTRY:			
YOUR COUNTRY:			

PARTNER Name:			
PARTNER Name:			
PARTNER Name:			

Answers on pg.133

SECRET #37: KIDS & RESPONSIBILITIES – BRAINSTORMING

This is an example of one way to teach children to take responsibility for SOME of the chores around the house.

1. Work with your group to BRAINSTORM ALL of the typical chores that need to be done in a WEEK. It's okay to include chores that children CAN'T do, such as cooking or driving. This makes it CLEAR to kids just how much work YOU are doing!

1.	2.	3.
4.	5.	6.
7.	8.	9.
10.	11.	12.
13.	14.	15.
16.	17.	18.
19.	20.	21.
22.	23.	24.
25.	26.	27.
28.	29.	30.
31.	32.	33.
34.	35.	36.
37.	38.	39.
40.	41.	42.
43.	44.	45.
46.	47.	48.

2. Now make a CALENDAR that includes ALL of these activities, divided appropriately between ALL of the members of the family (including Mom & Dad).

3. It's a good idea to LIMIT TIME for a chore to 10 min/day when you start. If it's not PERFECT, at least they're LEARNING!

4. You can buy ready-made "chore charts" on Amazon, download free customizable ones online, or make your own. It might look like this:

Answers on pg.134

SECRET #38: SENIORS WANT INDEPENDENCE – SURVEY ABOUT AGING PARENTS

Work with partners from 2 other countries. Try to GUESS the YES / NO ANSWERS about your partners' cultures. GUESS the right answer for CANADA. After everyone has guessed, share the results and see if you were right!

	PARTNER'S Name:	PARTNER'S Name:	
CHALLENGE:	COUNTRY:	COUNTRY:	**COUNTRY: CANADA**
1. Parents and even adult children live together all of their lives.			
2. Parents move in with their oldest son when they can't live independently.			
3. Parents move in with their oldest daughter when they can no longer live independently.			
4. Parents try to live independently until they die.			
5. Parents go to a government-funded retirement home.			
6. Parents go to a private retirement home, but it doesn't cost a lot.			
7. Parents go to a private retirement home, and it's VERY expensive.			
8. Other? (Your idea)			

Answers on pg. 135

SECRET #39: NOT A NUCLEAR FAMILY – The Story of Bob and Mary:
EXPLAINING A BLENDED FAMILY – READING COMPREHENSION

1. Once upon a time, **Bob** and **Mary** fell in love and got married. A few years later, **they had a daughter, Megan**, and a couple of years after that, **another daughter, Anna**.

Bob

Mary

Megan

Anna

2. Then, for reasons that are none of our business, Bob & Mary got a **divorce**. They decided on *joint custody* of the girls, which meant the girls spent half their time with Mary, and half their time with Bob.

Henry

Bob

Claudia

3. **Mary** met **Henry** online. Henry was **single**. They got **married** and **had a baby together, Leon.**

Leon

4. **Bob** met **Claudia** at work. **Claudia** had a son, **Miguel**, from a previous marriage. She has **full custody**, so Miguel lives with them full time.

Miguel

5. **With any luck, they'll all live HAPPILY EVER AFTER!**

SECRET #39: NOT A NUCLEAR FAMILY – EXPLAINING A BLENDED FAMILY:

How are they related *NOW*?

1. Bob is Mary's _____ and Mary is Bob's _____.

2. Megan and Anna are Bob's _____.

3. Miguel is Claudia's _____and Bob's _____. (son through remarriage)

4. Bob is Miguel's _____. (dad through remarriage)

5. Miguel is Megan and Anna's _____, and they are Miguel's

    _____. (siblings through marriage)

6. Claudia is Bob's _____.

7. Claudia is Megan and Anna's _____, and they are Claudia's

    _____

8. Miguel is _____ to Mary.

9. Leon is Mary and Henry's _____.

10. Leon is Megan and Anna's _____, and they are Leon's _____-

    _____ (same mother, different father).

11. Henry is Mary's _____ and Megan and Anna's _____-

    _____.

12. They are Henry's _____.

13. Leon is _____ to Bob or Claudia.

Answers on pg. 136

SECRET #40: LONE-PARENT FAMILIES – BRAINSTORMING – TRUE OR FALSE?

People tend to have a lot of PRECONCEPTIONS about what we used to call "single moms" or "single dads" (which is no longer Politically Correct), as well as about what kind of family life they have, and the effect of divorce on children. Of course, there are a LOT of variations, but do you think the following statements are mostly TRUE or FALSE in Canada?

1. Most lone-parent families are mothers and children.   _____

2. Lone-parent families tend to live in poverty.   _____

3. A lone-parent family is a "broken home".   _____

4. Children from a lone-parent family don't do well in school.   _____

5. Children from a lone-parent family get in trouble at school.   _____

6. Children from a lone-parent family are more likely to join a gang.   _____

7. Children from a lone-parent family are more likely to commit a crime.   _____

8. Children from a lone-parent family probably graduate from high school.   _____

9. Children from a lone-parent family probably graduate from university.   _____

10. Children from a lone-parent family go on to become professionals.   _____

11. Mothers and fathers in lone-parent families are more likely to use drugs.   _____

12. Mothers and fathers in lone-parent families are more likely to commit a crime   _____

13. Mothers and fathers in lone-parent families don't remarry.   _____

14. If mothers and fathers in lone-parent families do remarry, they will probably end up
    divorced.   _____

15. Mothers and fathers in lone-parent families have less education.   _____

16. Mothers and fathers in lone-parent families aren't professionals.   _____

Answers on pg. 137

SECRET #41: SEXUAL ACTIVITY AMONG TEENS – NO ACTIVITY

This is a VERY difficult topic to talk about. Most people born in Canada aren't comfortable talking about their children's sex lives, even though we tend to be liberal-minded in general. I think it's **unlikely** you will get your students to talk about sex, let alone teen sex.

NOTE: Every year, I do a morning session of **WOMEN ONLY** (I exchange my male students with another teacher's female students of an appropriate level of English.) During this "sex ed" class, we talk about as many issues related to female reproduction as the students request. Sometimes this provides an opportunity to discuss teen sex (but not always). One year, I invited a Public Health Nurse to present to the class on this day, but to my surprise, none of the students was willing to ask her ANYTHING. It turned out that they were more comfortable talking with ME about female issues.

With my own kids, my approach was to tell them they could ask me ANYTHING about sex (or anything else!) and that I would answer them HONESTLY. (I did not VOLUNTEER more information than they asked for, usually.)

Google: **Talking with Your Teens about Sex: Going Beyond "the Talk"** for a VERY good 4-page booklet on how to talk to teens about **safe sex**.

Some of the recommendations include:

- Talk about healthy, respectful relationships. ("No" means NO. – What is Consent?)

- Communicate your own expectations for your teen about relationships and sex.

- Provide factual information about ways to prevent HIV, STDs, and pregnancy (e.g., abstinence, condoms and contraception, and HIV/STD testing).

- Focus on the *benefits* of protecting oneself from HIV, STDs, and pregnancy.

- Provide information about where your teen can speak with a provider and receive sexual health services, such as HIV/STD testing

SECRET #42: VIRGINITY? – MAYBE NO ACTIVITY

(Same problem as #43.) Students are unlikely to be willing to talk about virginity except to insist that it is religiously or morally MANDATED.)

If you have a very small group of women who feel safe talking openly, you might try to initiate a discussion about this. One of the ways I approach touchy subjects is to pass out slips of paper, one per student (during the pandemic, if you using Zoom for classes as you know how to do Polls, you could Poll your students since the results are anonymous) to ask if they are interested in having a talk about a given subject, and only proceed if the majority say Yes.

For example, I offer a class (maybe once a year) where I will give a lesson about our "bad words". First, I survey the class to see if the majority are interested in this lesson (so far, they Always are!) Then I announce that we will be doing this lesson on the following Friday morning, for example (give a specific date and time), and let the students know that if they aren't comfortable attending this session, to let me know and I will mark them Present, even if they don't attend. I'm always surprised at how many students will attend this lesson!

So you could try a similar approach to the topic of virginity. I think we do need to discuss this topic, if possible, because of consequences such as "honour killings" – which DO happen in Canada (Google it!) – due to immigrants' daughters becoming 'too Canadian' and thinking that they have the right to choose what to do with their own bodies, despite the severe restrictions their culture puts on these choices.

They are a lot of wonderful resources available online to help you formulate lessons on the topic of virginity.

Google: talking to your kids about virginity

SECRET #43: GETTING ENGAGED – SURVEY

Work with partners from 2 other countries. Try to GUESS the YES / NO ANSWERS about your partners' cultures. GUESS the right answer for CANADA. After everyone has guessed, share the results and see if you were right!

	PARTNER'S Name:	PARTNER'S Name:	
CHALLENGE:	COUNTRY:	COUNTRY:	COUNTRY: **CANADA**
1. Marriages are often arranged.			
2. The bride & groom may meet for the first time at their wedding ceremony.			
3. Someone from the bride's or the groom's family may "represent" them. They may not attend their own wedding.			
4. Men and women aren't allowed to go out alone together (date) until they are married. (Need a chaperone)			
5. There is a BIG engagement party.			
6. Parents of the groom pay for the engagement party.			
7. When you get engaged, gifts are exchanged between the families of the bride-to-be & the groom-to-be. (How much $$?)			
8. Other? (Your idea)			

Answers on pg. 138

SECRET #44: WHO PAYS FOR THE WEDDING? – SURVEY

Survey your classmates, and fill in the following chart: If there is more than one person from a given country, check to see if they agree. If not, list the variations! Which country has the BIGGEST, MOST EXPENSIVE weddings? Where are weddings the SMALLEST or LEAST EXPENSIVE, on average?

COUNTRY	# OF GUESTS? RANGE: Least to Most	AVERAGE COST? (in $CDN)	WHO PAYS?

SECRET #45: WHO SHOULDN'T YOU INVITE (TO A WEDDING)? – SURVEY

List TYPES or GROUPS of people you wouldn't normally invite to a party or special event (not just weddings!), and give a REASON. Then decide HOW TRUE these rules are across the cultures in a) your group - b) in the class - & c) in Canada.

PEOPLE YOU SHOULDN'T INVITE TO A *WEDDING*:	WHY NOT?	% TRUE LIST BY COUNTRY
PEOPLE YOU SHOULDN'T INVITE TO A *PARTY*:	WHY NOT?	% TRUE LIST BY COUNTRY
PEOPLE YOU SHOULDN'T INVITE TO A *BBQ*:	WHY NOT?	% TRUE LIST BY COUNTRY
PEOPLE YOU SHOULDN'T INVITE TO A *PICNIC*:	WHY NOT?	% TRUE LIST BY COUNTRY

SECRET #45: WHO SHOULDN'T YOU INVITE? PRACTICE MAKING GENERALIZATIONS

Use this activity to practice the **GRAMMAR** of making **GENERALIZATIONS** as well as to recognize the **DANGER** of making generalizations.

There are certain words that signal or give us a clue to recognize generalizations.

• sometimes	• all (+ Plural noun)	• each (+ Singular noun)
• always	• a lot of	• every (+ Singular noun)
• never	• generally	• each and every (+ Singular noun)
• usually	• seldom	• almost always
• most	• few	• almost never
• many	• no (+ Singular noun)	• commonly (used in *writing*)

Exercise: Make sentences about <u>DOGS</u> that are GENERALIZATIONS using each of the above words. e.g., *Most dogs sleep 12-14 hours per day.*

1. Dogs sometimes _____

2. Dogs always _____

3. Dogs almost always _____

4. Dogs never _____

5. Dogs usually _____

6. Most dogs _____

7. Many dogs _____

8. All dogs _____

9. A lot of dogs _____

10. Generally, dogs _____

11. Dogs seldom _____

12. No dog ever _____

13. Few dogs _____

14. Most of the dogs I know _____

15. Dogs almost never _____

SECRET #46: SAME-SEX PARENTS: CONVERSATION ABOUT ADOPTION

In small groups, discuss some of the following questions about orphans and adoption in your country of birth. It's okay to use the internet to gather data.

1. What are the views of adoption in your country of birth?

2. How common is it?

3. One of the reasons for adoption in Canada is infertility issues. Is this increasing in your country of birth?

4. Approximately how many orphans or abandoned babies are there in your country of birth right now?

5. What is the ratio of boys to girls?

6. Where do orphans usually live?

7. Is adoption common?

8. How complicated is it to adopt a child?

9. How expensive is it to adopt a child?

10. What is the difference between domestic and international adoption?

11. How common is it for people from other countries to adopt children from your country of birth?

12. Do you know anyone who is adopted?

13. Do you know anyone who has adopted a child?

14. What are some of the reasons people choose to adopt?

15. If you were unable to have your own children, would you consider adopting? Why or why not?

SECRET #47: DIVORCE IS COMMON – DIGITAL DECISION-MAKING

One of the reasons that "PROS" and "CONS" lists don't usually WORK is that sometimes, 1 PRO = 5 CONS (or vice-versa). This technique – done with a PARTNER – helps you to figure out your PRIORITIES when making a decision.

(This technique works well for *ANY* kind of decision, when you are unable to decide because PROs and CONs don't WORK.)

DIGITAL DECISION-MAKING CHART

STEP 1: Think of 5 reasons to STAY MARRIED, and 5 reasons to GET A DIVORCE. Write them down in the left-hand column, *IN ANY ORDER.*

10 FACTORS (in any order)	1.	2.	3.	4.	5.	6.	7.	8.	9.	10.	TOTALs
1.											
2.											
3.											
4.											
5.											
6.											
7.											
8.											
9.											
10.											

SECRET #47: DIGITAL DECISION-MAKING

STEP 2: Have your partner read only 2 choices at a time, and you must tell him or her *INSTANTLY* which reason is *more important*.

Let's say your list looks like this:

TOP 10 (in any order)	1.	2.	3.	4.	5.	6.	7.	8.	9.	10.	TOTALs
1. Good cook		1	3								
2. Good with the kids			3								
3. Hits me											

ANSWERING **PARTNER: When your partner says, "What's more important, good cook or good with the kids?" and you must QUICKLY choose one of them.**

ASKING **PARTNER: Ask your partner 1. vs. 2: "What's more important, good cook or good with the kids?" If he or she says, "good cook", write the number 1 under the 2. along the top of the chart. If he or she says, "good with the kids", write the number 2 under the 2. along the top of the chart. *NEVER write ANYTHING in the grey spaces!***

Then ask your partner 1. vs. 3. "What's more important, good cook or hits me?" If he or she says, "good cook", write the number 1 under the 3. along the top of the chart. . If he or she says, "hits me", write the number 3 under the 3. along the top of the chart.

Continuing asking 1 vs. 4, 1 vs. 5, 1 vs. 6, 1 vs. 7, 1 vs. 8, 1 vs. 9, & 1 vs. 10 and write their choice in the FIRST ROW of the chart.

Then ask 2 vs. 3, 2 vs. 4, 2 vs. 5, etc. and write their choice in the SECOND ROW of the chart. Continue with each reason until you have compared values for ALL of the 10 reasons listed. You should have filled up ALL the white spaces in the chart.

(See the next page for an example of how a completed chart might look.)

*** *When you've done this for one partner, SWITCH ROLES and go through the other partner's chart.*

SECRET #47: SAMPLE DIGITAL DECISION MAKING CHART

TOP 10 (in any order)	1.	2.	3.	4.	5.	6.	7.	8.	9.	10.	TOTALs
1. good cook		2	3	4	5	1	1	8	1	10	3
2. good with the kids			3	2	5	2	2	2	2	2	7
3. hits me				3	3	3	3	3	3	3	9
4. drinks too much					5	4	7	4	4	4	5
5. good job						5	5	5	5	10	7
6. snores							7	8	6	10	1
7. embarrassed to be divorced								7	7	10	7
8. makes me laugh									8	10	3
9. is good looking										10	0
10. I'm lonely											6

Now add up the TOTAL number of times you see the # 1, # 2, # 3, etc. ANYWHERE in the table & put it into the Totals Column. So if you see the number 3 NINE times, this is his or her TOP *PRIORITY!* If 2-3 #s are the same, CHOOSE which one is MORE important. For example, 3 of these choices came up 7 times.

Then write the reasons that you chose *most frequently* the TOP 10 as #1 etc. below.

1. _____ hits me _X = BAD_____ (chose this 9 times) _____

2. _____ good with the kids = GOOD_____ This is a **HIGH PRIORITY**, but *doesn't* outweigh the *negative* of "hits me" _____

3. _____ **embarrassed to be divorced** - given as a reason to stay married, but is essentially _____ X = BAD _____

4. _____ good job = GOOD _____ = Important, but **NOT** as important as #s 1-3

5. _____ drinks too much _____ X = BAD _____ (but **can he/she CHANGE?**)_____

This DOESN'T make your decisions for you, but should help you sort out your priorities.

SECRET #47: DIGITAL DECISION MAKING

MY TOP 10 PRIORITIES IN MAKING THIS DECISION:

1. _____

2. _____

3. _____

4. _____

5. _____

6. _____

7. _____

8. _____

9. _____

10. _____

NOTE: Your <u>TOP 5 PRIORITIES</u> are the MOST IMPORTANT ONES.

SECRET #48: KIDS – WHO GETS CUSTODY? ROLE-PLAYING A COURT CASE

Divide the class into 2 teams – "In favour of Joint Custody" and "In favour of Full Custody to Mary". Give the teams 15-20 minutes to prepare their case, using the following details. Teams can make up any additional details that they want. Tell them to use their creativity – they want their client to WIN! You can be the judge.

FACTS of the CASE:

- Bob and Mary have been married for 12 years.

- Bob is an accountant who earns $140,000 per year.

- They have 2 daughters, Megan – who is now 9 – and Anna – who is 6.

- Mary was a stay-at-home mom until Anna started school full time last year, and then she went back to her job as a loans officer in a bank.

- She earns $45,000 per year.

- A few months ago, Bob moved out and got his own townhouse, stating the "the marriage had gone stale".

- Mary is currently living in the matrimonial home with the 2 girls.

- Bob is still paying the mortgage payments - $2,400 per month – and the taxes, $7,500 per year.

- Mary has been paying for the utilities and food.

- In addition to paying the mortgage & taxes, Bob has been giving Mary $1,900 per month to help support his daughters.

- However, he has only been seeing the girls on the weekends, and he is unhappy about this.

- He would like Joint Custody. He wants the girls to stay with him for 2 weeks, and then with their mother for 2 weeks. He lives close enough that they won't have to change schools when they're with him.

- If he gets joint custody, he is sure his living expenses will increase, and he plans to reduce his child support payments to $1,000 per month (though he has agreed to continue to pay the mortgage & taxes).

- Mary is insisting that she keep full custody of the girls. She thinks that as soon as Bob gets a girlfriend, he will hand the responsibility for the girls onto this other woman. She says that Bob has never had full responsibility for the girls and she doesn't trust him to raise them as she wants them raised.

SECRET #49: PAYING CHILD SUPPORT – SURVEY

Work with partners from 2 other countries. Try to GUESS the YES / NO ANSWERS about your partners' cultures. GUESS the right answer for CANADA. After everyone has guessed, share the results and see if you were right!

	PARTNER'S Name:	PARTNER'S Name:	
CHALLENGE:	COUNTRY:	COUNTRY:	COUNTRY: **CANADA**
1. Divorce is legal / acceptable.			
2. After a divorce, the mother usually gets custody.			
3. After a divorce, the father usually gets custody.			
4. After a divorce, the father must pay child support.			
5. Child support is mandatory by law.			
6. The government sets out the amount of the payment.			
7. The wife has to pay taxes on child support payments.			
8. Other? (Your idea)			

Answers on pg. 139

SECRET #50: "PLAYING NICE" WITH YOUR EX – ROLE-PLAY

Work in groups of 4. Imagine that you are attending a school event with your new spouse, and you run into your ex with his/her new spouse.

Write a 4-part DIALOGUE to practice making SMALL TALK about the weather, the school, the child and even a pet. Make sure all 4 people act "nice" to each other. The dialogue should continue for 5-10 minutes. Get CREATIVE! (Sometimes we just PRETEND to be nice to each other ...)

Let's say the 4 people are: Bob & his new wife Claudia, Bob's ex, Mary, and her new husband Henry.

You can begin something like this:

Bob: Oh, hi Mary. Mary, have you met my wife Claudia?

Mary: (Shaking hands) Hi, Claudia, nice to meet you.

Claudia: Hi, Mary, nice to meet you, too.

Mary: Henry, this is my ex-husband Bob and his wife, Claudia.

Henry: (Shaking hands) Hi, Bob, Claudia, nice to meet you.

Mary: (Speaking to Claudia) Have you been to this school before?

Claudia: Yes, Bob and I came here for the "Meet the Teacher event in September. It's a lovely school, isn't it?"

etc. etc.

WRITE your 4-part DIALOGUE. Practice your dialogue a few times, and then present it to the class.

_____

_____

_____

_____

_____

_____

_____

SECRET #51: WORK vs. "ME" (FREE) TIME – CONVERSATION

In small groups, discuss some of the following questions:

1. In your country of birth, how is housework divided between men, women & children?

2. Are a mother's responsibilities today greater than her mother's were, or less?

3. Are a mother's responsibilities today greater than her grandmother's were, or less?

4. Did your mother work outside the home? If yes, was it full time or part time? (If she lived on a farm, this counts as full-time work, since she had many responsibilities in addition to caring for her home and family.)

5. Did your grandmother work outside the home? If yes, was it full-time or part-time?

6. Did you work full time before you came to Canada?

7. Do women in your country of birth typically work full time after they have children?

8. Are there "pink' jobs (chores done primarily by women) and "blue" jobs (chores done primarily by men? If so, explain which chores are done by each gender.

9. Research shows that women who don't get some "down" time (time to themselves, with no responsibilities) each day tend to suffer from depression and anxiety. Why do you think this is?

10. When you get some free time, what do you enjoy doing?

11. How often do you get to do this activity?

12. Psychologists recommend that busy mothers SCHEDULE some "me" time (even 15 minutes) every day. How can you arrange this?

13. Do fathers also need some "me" time?

14. How can they arrange for this?

SECRET #52: HOW TO SUCCEED IN SCHOOL – HOW HARD DO PEOPLE REALLY WORK? – SURVEY

Survey your classmates, and fill in the following chart: If there is more than one person from a given country, check to see if they agree. If not, list the variations! Which country has the most RELAXED ATTITUDE about working CONTINUOUSLY while a work? Which country has the most stringent work ethic?

COUNTRY	Does your country have a strong WORK ETHIC?	In an 8-hour shift, how many hours do people goof off?	What jobs offer more free time?

SECRET #53: ACTIVE LEARNING – SELF-REFLECTION & CONVERSATION

How I Learn New Things:
Check ALL that apply to you. Add more ideas if you can. With your group, DISCUSS how you learn BEST. Share your favourite experience of learning something new!

☐ A friend showed me how.

☐ I watched YouTube videos again and again for more instructions.

☐ I had to practice a lot.

☐ I had to undo it and redo it many times.

☐ I like to experiment, even if I fail.

☐ I like to follow directions.

☐ I refuse to give up.

☐ I figure it out myself.

☐ I Google it.

☐ I like to learn from experience.

☐ I prefer to learn by trial and error.

☐ It takes time. I have to remember to be patient.

OTHER WAYS?

☐ _____

☐ _____

☐ _____

☐ _____

☐ _____

SECRET #53: ACTIVE LEARNING – LATERAL THINKING EXERCISE

Lateral thinking puzzles are a common way to stretch our minds. Try to come up with as many possible solutions to this RIDDLE as you can. (You can be as SILLY & IMAGINATIVE as you WANT!)

RIDDLE: Can you EXPLAIN this?

- 6 people are in the kitchen
- There is a basket on the counter with 6 eggs in it
- Each person takes an egg
- *When everyone has taken an egg, there is 1 egg in the basket.*

HOW CAN THIS BE?

POSSIBLE SOLUTIONS:
1.
2.
3.
4.
5.
6.
7.
8.
9.
10.
11.
12.

Answers on pg. 140

SECRET #54: PARENTS ARE TEACHERS – CHILDREN'S LEARNING STYLES QUIZ

1. You let your child pick out one new toy. Which toy are they most likely to choose?
- a) Art set
- b) Play microphone
- c) Hula hoop or soccer ball

2. Your child's favourite after-school activity:
- a) Art lessons
- b) Music lessons
- c) Sports or drama lessons

3. If there is a 10-minute wait for something, how does your child occupy him/herself?
- a) Drawing or watching YouTubes
- b) Talking your ear off or listening to music
- c) Digging in your purse while bouncing in place

4. Which family activity is your child most likely to choose?
- a) A movie / video
- b) Singing together
- c) A sports activity or a video game

5. When your child reads a book to himself, he:
- a) Sits quietly – may not hear you when you speak to him/her
- b) Mouths the words aloud or asks you to read it to him
- c) Fidgets, paces or runs his/her finger along the page

6. Which of these computer activities is your child most drawn to?
- a) Looking at photos / drawings / art
- b) Listening to music
- c) Playing a video game

Mostly A's = a VISUAL learner – Learns by LOOKING

- Make lists, charts, graphs, and diagrams.
- Use COLOUR! He or she can write spelling words or important details in different colours or use different-coloured highlighters (for younger kids, use scented markers)
- Give your visual kid OBJECTS to help him/her think through MATH problems. (If I had 10 raisins and Mom ate 2, how many are left?)

Mostly B's = an AUDITORY learner – Learns by LISTENING

- Only about 10% of kids are auditory learners
- Give verbal instructions and study for tests by repeating information verbally – like a "spelling bee"
- Give him/her a voice recorder / app: Saying things aloud can help him/her retain info, and re-playing the recording boosts comprehension even more.
- Turn a book into a puppet show & he/she'll remember the story.

Mostly C's = a KINESTHETIC learner – Learns by DOING

- *Most (especially young) kids absorb information best when they're physically engaged*
- Many kinesthetic learners have trouble sitting still for long stretches.
- Turn homework into a sporting event: let him/her catch a foam ball from around the room each time he/she answers a question correctly or give him/her a squishy toy to squeeze and manipulate.

The most COMMON learning style is Visual-Kinesthetic – *SEE it and DO it TOGETHER*
- Help the child to make his/her own FLASH CARDS

SECRET #55: COMMUNICATE WITH THE TEACHER – WRITING EMAILS

Write short, appropriate responses to the following emails. Make sure to include a *SPECIFIC* subject line!

#1:   To: awesomeparents@gmail.com
        From: Chris Yu <chrisyu@bestschool.ca>
        Subject: "Me to We" Event - Thur. Nov 12 @ 7 pm

Hi Parents! I just wanted to remind you that we are having our annual "Me to We" event this Thursday. All of the children have prepared skits and songs to show their Best School spirit, and to help raise funds for our charity in Africa. Tickets are $7 per Person, or $15 for the Family. Please RSVP to let me know if you can come, and how many tickets you'd like.

Chris

YOUR RESPONSE: Subject: _____

***

#2:   To: urkdwazhrt@gmail.com
        From: Chris Yu <chrisyu@bestschool.ca>
        Subject:_bullying incident

Dear Mr. and Mrs. Urkdwazhrt, I'm sorry to tell you that your daughter Janice has been the victim of a bullying incident today. Janice had a book that one of the other girls wanted, and the girl pulled the book roughly out of Janice's hands, causing her to get a small paper cut on her left hand, which required a Band-Aid. The girl apologized, but congruent with our "Zero Tolerance" policy on bullying, she has received a 1-day suspension. Please call me at 905-555-3322 to arrange a time to speak with me about the incident.

Chris

YOUR RESPONSE: Subject: _____

Answers on pg. 141

SECRET #56: UNDERSTANDING REPORT CARDS – BRAINSTORMING

Look at the Sample Report Card COMMENTS below, and try to guess what mark (A, B, C, D,) the child received in each subject.

1. Most of the time, Akim successfully makes inferences by predicting relevant events when reading non-fiction texts. During class, he was consistently able to predict outcomes by using the title page of Volcanoes of the World and photos in the text Forest Animals. At home, when reading the newspaper, Akim could further build his excellent inferring skills by making predictions from the headlines.

Probable Mark in this Subject? _____

2. In Number Sense and Numeration, John needs direct assistance in order to apply the correct operation (e.g. addition or subtraction) when solving problems. He is able to add and subtract 2-digit numbers, using manipulatives and on his whiteboard. However, when solving tasks in his math journal, John needs help to re-examine the problem, highlighting key words to help him choose the correct operation.

Probable Mark in this Subject? _____

3. Rebecca is able to follow and give basic classroom instructions such as Comment ça va? and Quel temps fait-il? She experienced a bit of difficulty in giving an oral presentation on an assigned topic. Rebecca is encouraged to use available resources and seek feedback from the teacher and her peers. Rebecca reads a simple story and is able to give brief oral responses. In her oral response to the story "Au zoo", Rebecca used pictures to help with comprehension. She would benefit from an opportunity to read short texts and restate them in her own words. Rebecca is usually able to write simple, short sentences on assigned topics.

Probable Mark in this Subject? _____

4. When reading stories with unfamiliar words, Janice is sometimes unable to retell the main ideas from the story due to challenges with reading fluency. With some help, she is able to orally retell ideas from stories (e.g., My Favourite Pet) that use familiar words from the classroom word wall (e.g., dog, cat, fish, home). Janice should practice looking at the whole sentence and reading it out loud to help her understand the meaning of unfamiliar words.

Probable Mark in this Subject? _____

Answers on pg. 142

SECRET #57: HOW MUCH HOMEWORK? – SURVEY

Try to GUESS the answer for each country before you ask! Then survey your classmates, and fill in the following chart: If there is more than one person from a given country, check to see if they agree. If not, list the variations! Which country gives the MOST HOMEWORK? Which country has the LEAST?

COUNTRY	How much homework do kids get in Elementary School?	How much homework do kids get in High School?	How much homework do kids get in College or University?	How much homework do KIDS get in Canada?

SECRET #58: VOLUNTEER AT YOUR CHILD'S SCHOOL – READING COMPREHENSION

Read the following paragraph about the benefits of volunteering. Answer the questions IN POINT FORM and then DISCUSS this topic with a partner or small group.

In addition to providing a valuable reference for future work, research shows that volunteering offers us important psychological and even physical health benefits. For those who suffer from depression, focusing outside of ourselves is a great way to lower our stress and increase feelings of self-worth. It helps us feel connected to our community, and this is especially important when we have moved into a new culture or community. Often, volunteering offers the chance to make new friends, both in clients and co-workers. Volunteering can not only make us happier, it also can add years to our lives, possibly by lowering our stress. There are a number of organizations that will help match you with an appropriate volunteer opportunity. It isn't always working in a hospital! Finally, volunteering will give you a chance to practice your English, learn new hard and soft skills (see Secret #68) and gain valuable Canadian work experience.

COMPREHENSION QUESTIONS:

1. Name 3 psychological benefits of volunteering that are mentioned in the text.

   _____   _____   _____

2. How can volunteering help us to live longer?

   _____

3. When is volunteering particularly important?

   _____

4. Name 3 ways that volunteering can help you get a job.

   _____   _____   _____

INFERENCES:

5. Why does the text mention that volunteering isn't always in a hospital?

   _____

   _____

6. Why does the author mention self-worth?

   _____

   _____

7. Does this text offer a balanced view of the effects of volunteering?

   _____

Answers on pg. 143

SECRET #59: LEARN PHRASAL VERBS – VERBS with "OFF"

Match the following idioms to their correct meaning.

1. to fall off (business)		a) to criticize someone harshly
2. to doze off		b) "I don't believe you! Are you kidding?"
3. to go off (alarm)		c) to leave suddenly
4. to tell someone off		d) to drop suddenly
5. to pull s/thing off (positive)		e) to emit (fumes or gasses)
6. to come off		f) to fall asleep inappropriately
7. to stay off		g) to begin to make loud sounds
8. to take off		h) to not walk or sit on something
9. to give off		i) to succeed (but surprised)
10. Come off it!"		j) to become detached from something

EXERCISE: Replace the UNDERLINED with the best idiom from the above list. Make sure to use the *CORRECT TENSE!*

1. I am sick and tired of my neighbour letting her dog do its business on my lawn. I have asked her nicely. Now I am going to <u>yell at her about it.</u>

2. I don't know what happened to Akim. One minute he was here, and the next, he had <u>left suddenly</u>.

3. Sales of our new produce have <u>dropped suddenly</u> this quarter.

4. It's hard for me to stay awake when I'm studying. I keep <u>falling asleep when I shouldn't</u>.

5. "You want me to lend you more money? <u>I don't believe you</u>!"

6. We thought the customer hated our presentation, but in the end, we <u>were successful</u>.

7. "I just washed the kitchen floor. Please <u>avoid walking on it until it dries</u>."

8. It is dangerous to use spray paint without a mask because it <u>emits</u> dangerous fumes.

9. About two weeks after I bought my new car, the hub cap <u>separated from the wheel of my car</u>.

10. I hate my smoke detector sometimes. It <u>rings loudly</u> every time I fry something!

Answers on pg. 119

SECRET #60: CANADIAN CREDENTIALS – INTERNET RESEACH

Google: _____ **(choose 3 possible careers in Canada)**

e.g., <u>hairdresser occupation Canada</u> – click on the <u>jobbank.gc.ca</u> link

Fill in the following chart with the following information.

	CAREER POSSIBILITY #1	CAREER POSSIBILITY #2	CAREER POSSIBILITY #3
SUMMARY			
DESCRIPTION			
WAGES			
OUTLOOK			
REQUIRMENTS			
JOBS in YOUR REGION			
SKILLS			

SECRET #61: PROFESSIONAL DEVELOPMENT (PD) – BRAINSTORMING & SURVEY

STEP #1: With your group, BRAINSTORM 10 OCCUPATIONS where PD is EXTREMELY important and 10 occupations where it shouldn't matter as much.

PD = EXTREMELY IMPORTANT		PD = NOT VERY IMPORTANT	
1.		1.	
2.		2.	
3.		3.	
4.		4.	
5.		5.	
6.		6.	
7.		7.	
8.		8.	
9.		9.	
10.		10.	

STEP #2: SURVEY your classmates, or Google: _____ (name of occupation) professional development Canada – to see if you were RIGHT about how important PD is considered for each occupation. Put a ✔ beside the occupation if your guess was <u>correct</u>, and an X if your guess was <u>incorrect</u>.

SECRET #62: DIFFERENCES IN FINDING A JOB – SURVEY

Work with partners from 2 other countries. Try to GUESS the YES / NO ANSWERS about your partners' cultures. GUESS the right answer for CANADA. After everyone has guessed, share the results and see if you were right!

	PARTNER'S Name:	PARTNER'S Name:	
CHALLENGE:	**COUNTRY:**	**COUNTRY:**	**COUNTRY: CANADA**
1. You don't need a resume for most jobs.			
2. You put your age on your resume.			
3. You put your health condition on your resume.			
4. You put your marital status on your resume.			
5. You put your photo on your resume.			
6. You use the SAME resume to apply to ALL jobs.			
7. You must put your legal name on a resume.			
8. Other? (Your idea)			

Answers on pg. 144

SECRET #63: VOLUNTEERING (GET CANADIAN EXPERIENCE!) – CONVERSATION

In small groups, discuss some of the following questions:

1. What do you think the word "volunteer" means?

2. Check a dictionary. Were you right?

3. The Oxford Learner's Dictionary defines "volunteer" as: *to offer to do something without being forced to do it or without getting paid for it.* Does this match your original definition?

4. Is volunteering common in your country of birth? Why or why not?

5. Do you think volunteering is a sign of an affluent country?

6. Have you ever volunteered within your community (in your country of birth or Canada?)

   - If yes, how many hours per week / month did/do you volunteer?

   - What did you do?

7. Have you ever volunteered at home?

   - If yes, what did you do? (Help with childcare or caring for elderly relatives, help with cooking or cleaning, etc.)

   - How many hours per week / month did/do you volunteer?

   - Did you **really** volunteer, or were you '***volunteered'*** by someone? Who?

   - Would you consider a "stay-at-home mom or dad" a volunteer?

   - Would you consider children who help their parents with the chores to be volunteering?

8. Why do you think volunteering is considered almost equal to paid work when applying for jobs in Canada? (This isn't true in the United States, in general.)

9. Where can you find more information on finding a volunteer job in your community?

SECRET #64: BUILDING YOUR NETWORK – INTERNET RESEARCH

As a CLASS, BRAINSTORM 8 places where you could build your network (meet people with similar business or career interests). Divide into teams of 2-3. Each team will search for the address of ONE network-building place in your town.

When you're done, share your information with the rest of the class.

TYPICAL PLACE TO BUILD YOUR NETWORK	ADDRESS of a place like this in our town. (Also provide contact phone number, dates & times & any costs, if possible.)
1.	
2.	
3.	
4.	
5.	
6.	
7.	
8.	

SECRET #65: SHOW SELF-CONFIDENCE – BRAINSTORM YOUR ELEVATOR PITCH

How do you respond to the request in a job interview, "Tell me about yourself"?

Step #1: Watch this YouTube: Elevator Pitch for Job Seekers – How to answer "Tell me about yourself" in an interview

Step #2: Answer these questions to help you PREPARE:

1. Who are you & what do you do? Name, key credentials & experience

_____

_____

2. Why should they care? (What have you got to OFFER? What makes you INTERESTING or SPECIAL? Tell them a SPECIFIC skill or accomplishment.)

_____

_____

3. What are YOU looking for? Why are you interested in working for THIS company? (HINT: Show that you KNOW something about the company. Check out their Mission Statement or Corporate Philosophy/Goals – and tell them how this is a good fit for you.)

_____

_____

Step #3: Write a 30-second pitch!

SECRET #66: STATUTORY HOLIDAYS – INTERNET RESEARCH

Google: statutory holidays _____ **(your province or territory)**

Fill in the following chart with this information.

HOLIDAY	DATE

What are some other special days celebrated in your province or territory?

HOLIDAY	DATE

SECRET #67: DIVERSITY AT WORK – SURVEY

Try to **GUESS** the answer for each country before you ask! Then survey your classmates, and fill in the following chart: If there is more than one person from a given country, check to see if they agree. If not, list the variations! Which country has the **HIGHEST PERCENT OF MINORITIES?** Which country has the **LOWEST?**

COUNTRY	How many different visible minorities do you have?	Do visible minorities have EQUAL access to opportunity (like getting HIRED)?	Do visible minorities earn less?	Is racism a problem in this country?
CANADA				

Answers on pg. 145

SECRET #68: SPEAK UP IN MEETINGS – IDENTIFYING HARD & SOFT SKILLS

Mark the following skills as "H" for Hard Skills (*teachable* abilities or skills) or "S" for Soft Skills (*personal attributes, interpersonal skills, communication skills & understanding social cues*)

accounting		adaptability		administration	
analysis		attitude		automotive	
banking		bookkeeping		carpentry	
communication		computer hardware		conflict resolution.	
construction		creative thinking		critical thinking	
data management		decision making		design	
editing		electrical		engineering	
financial		flexibility		healthcare	
information technology		languages		legal	
manufacturing		math		medical	
mediation		motivation		networking	
nursing		pharmaceutical		pipefitter	
plumbing		positivity		problem-solving	
programming		project management		research	
science		software design		spreadsheets	
teaching		teamwork		telecommunications	
testing		time management		translation	
word processing		work ethic		writing	

Answers on pg. 146

SECRET #69: BE PUNCTUAL – WHO HAS TO BE ON TIME? – BRAINSTORMING

Different occupations – in different cultures – and even different roles within a company – may have VERY different expectations about punctuality.

ALL OF THE FOLLOWING EMPLOYEES ARE TYPICALLY LATE.

In small groups, look at the following scenarios and decide YES or NO. Which employee is likely to be in trouble, and whose job is probably safe despite their lack of punctuality?
NOTE: there are NO "correct answers" to this! *YOU* decide.

---

1. BOB = Safe? ☐ YES ☐ NO

Bob works in pharmaceutical sales. He has worked with this company for 3 months. He has about 3-4 appointments per day with physicians or their staff, where he presents updated information about the drugs that his company produces. He also has weekly and monthly sales meetings with his colleagues and supervisor.

---

2. JANICE = Safe? ☐ YES ☐ NO

Janice is a bank teller. She is friendly, as well as extremely accurate. Her cash is never over or under what it should be. She has been working for the bank for 5 years.

---

3. EUN YOUNG = Safe? ☐ YES ☐ NO

Eun Young is the Head Chef in a famous Korean restaurant which is working on achieving a Michelin star. There are 12 kitchen staff working under her. She has worked there for 5 years.

---

4. George Yi = Safe? ☐ YES ☐ NO

George Yi is a computer programmer for Ying Xie Video Games. He is a talented programmer, but his lateness is delaying release of a new game. He has been with the company for 3 years.

---

5. AKIM = Safe? ☐ YES ☐ NO

Akim is a graphic designer who is also a Team Leader for the Packaging Team at a large graphic design company. Akim and his team have won a number of awards for their work, and their customers rave about them, but the company just hired a new manager who is a stickler for punctuality.

SECRET #70: BE HONEST – WHEN DO WE TELL THE (WHOLE) TRUTH? – SURVEY

Work with partners from 2 other countries. Try to GUESS the <u>FREQUENCY</u> (ALWAYS / USUALLY / SOMETIMES / NEVER) about your partners' cultures and for CANADA. After everyone has guessed, discuss the results.

CHALLENGE:	PARTNER'S Name: COUNTRY:	PARTNER'S Name: COUNTRY:	COUNTRY: **CANADA**
1. People tell the truth to their parents.			
2. People tell the truth to their spouse.			
3. People tell the truth to their best friend.			
4. People tell the truth to their boss.			
5. People tell the truth to their clients or customers.			
6. People tell the truth to insurance companies.			
7. People tell the truth to the police.			
8. People tell the truth to the government.			
9. People tell the truth to the media.			
10. Other? (Your idea)			

Answers on pg. 147

SECRET #71: RESPECT YOUR BOSS – WHAT MAKES A GOOD BOSS? – SURVEY

As a CLASS, BRAINSTORM 8 characteristics that would make someone a good boss. Then break into small groups and try to GUESS if this would be considered TRUE for a boss in other people's country of birth. How about in Canada?

CHARACTERISTICS OF A GOOD BOSS:	PARTNER'S Name: COUNTRY:	PARTNER'S Name: COUNTRY:	COUNTRY: CANADA
1.			
2.			
3.			
4.			
5.			
6.			
7.			
8.			

Answers on pg. 148

SECRET #72: LEARN THE JARGON – JOB-SEEKING JARGON – MATCHING

Match the following common terms for job seekers to their correct meaning. After you've checked your answers, discuss what these terms mean in your country of birth or in Canada (if you have experience job-seeking here).

JOB-SEEKING TERMS		MEANING
1. Background Check		a) full-time employment or full-time equivalent
2. Benefits		b) job openings that aren't advertised (which is the MAJORITY of job openings in Canada)
3. Corporate Culture		c) skills from previous jobs or training which you will be able to easily apply to your next position
4. Curriculum Vitae (CV)		d) meeting with a contact to simply learn more about a company or an industry (often leads to a job!)
5. Fit		e) individuals/companies that are hired to find qualified candidates for specific positions
6. FTE		f) verify the information an applicant provides
7. Hidden Job Market		g) from health and dental insurance to paid vacations, sick leave, child care, pension plans, etc.
8. Informational Interview		h) similar to a resume; usually used for professions
9. Job Shadowing		i) how well a candidate meets the job requirements and how well he/she would mesh with the company culture
10. Keywords		j) expectations, values and rules of conduct that are shared and maintained by a company and its employees
11. Recruiters or Headhunters		k) spending a short time observing someone while they're working so you can see what's involved
12. Transferable Skills		l) terms for which recruiters and HR managers might scan a resume

Answers on pg. 149

SECRET #73: OBEY THE BOSS – BUT DO WE? – SURVEY

Try to guess WHAT PERCENT of the following statements are TRUE for each country before you ask (4 columns = 100%) Then survey your classmates, and fill in the following chart: If there is more than one person from a given country, check to see if they agree. If not, list the variations! Which country is MOST LIKELY to obey the boss? Which country is the LEAST LIKELY?

COUNTRY	Employees ALWAYS obey their boss	Employees obey their boss most of the time	Employees disobey the boss when they think they can get away with it	Employees enjoy rebelling against bosses
Canada	40% (Canadians tend to be fairly rule-obeying)	30% (If we think a rule or order is STUPID, we may not obey it)	20% (especially in lower-paying jobs)	10% (mostly teens & young people)

SECRET #74: YOU NEED A MENTOR – BUT WHY? – BRAINSTORMING

In a small group, BRAINSTORM 8 benefits of having a Career or Business MENTOR – and then think of an OCCUPATION where it MATTERS. When you're done, COMPARE your list with the rest of the class.

BENEFITS OF HAVING A MENTOR	Name an OCCUPATION where this might be ESPECIALLY helpful.
1.	
2.	
3.	
4.	
5.	
6.	
7.	
8.	

Answers on pg.150

SECRET #75: TEACH THEM ABOUT YOUR CULTURE – GROUP BRAINSTORMING & PRESENTATIONS – "5 THINGS YOU SHOULD KNOW ABOUT _____"

STEP #1: Elicit "5 things everyone should know about CANADA" (my list is below).

STEP #2: Break students into groups according to country or region (if there is only one person from a given country, they can work alone or choose to work with people who may share the same religion or a similar culture.

STEP #3: USING *FLIP-CHART PAPER*, have each group fill out "5 Things You Should Know About _____" (their country)

STEP #4: Have each group do a MINI-PRESENTATION on the things in their chart (during the SAME CLASS – don't give them time to WORRY about this!)

STEP #5: Using the template on the NEXT PAGE, have the rest of the class TAKE NOTES during the presentations.

This activity has been very successful, even with a BASIC class!

FIVE THINGS EVERYONE SHOULD KNOW ABOUT <u>CANADA</u>	FIVE THINGS EVERYONE SHOULD KNOW ABOUT _____
1. Terry Fox 2. Insulin was invented here 3. Basketball was invented by a Canadian 4. Ryan Reynolds, Jim Carrey, Rachel McAdams were born here 5. Most educated country in the world!	1. _____ 2. _____ 3. _____ 4. _____ 5. _____
FIVE THINGS EVERYONE SHOULD KNOW ABOUT _____	FIVE THINGS EVERYONE SHOULD KNOW ABOUT _____
1. _____ 2. _____ 3. _____ 4. _____ 5. _____	1. _____ 2. _____ 3. _____ 4. _____ 5. _____

SECRET #75: 5 THINGS YOU SHOULD KNOW ABOUT MY COUNTRY OF BIRTH:

FIVE THINGS EVERYONE SHOULD

KNOW ABOUT _____

1. _____
2. _____
3. _____
4. _____
5. _____

FIVE THINGS EVERYONE SHOULD

KNOW ABOUT _____

1. _____
2. _____
3. _____
4. _____
5. _____

FIVE THINGS EVERYONE SHOULD

KNOW ABOUT _____

1. _____
2. _____
3. _____
4. _____
5. _____

FIVE THINGS EVERYONE SHOULD

KNOW ABOUT _____

1. _____
2. _____
3. _____
4. _____
5. _____

FIVE THINGS EVERYONE SHOULD

KNOW ABOUT _____

1. _____
2. _____
3. _____
4. _____
5. _____

FIVE THINGS EVERYONE SHOULD

KNOW ABOUT _____

1. _____
2. _____
3. _____
4. _____
5. _____

SECRET #76: K.I.S.S. – KEEP IT SHORT & SWEET – WRITING EMAILS

Write short, friendly responses to the following emails. *Make sure to include a GREAT subject line!*

#1: To: allstaff@awesomestuff.com
From: Chris Yu <hr@awesomestuff.com>
Subject: staff meeting attendance

To all staff – It has come to our attention that many staff members are not attending our quarterly "Where Are We Now?" staff events. Most of the staff members who bother to RSVP have not actually shown up for the actual events! We're hearing what you aren't saying, so now we're asking for your suggestions: What would give you better incentive to attend the next event? (We can't hold it in Florida in February, sorry … LOL)

Chris

YOUR RESPONSE: Subject: _____

***

#2: To: yuyuyu@gmail.com
From: ChrisYu2@gmail.com
Subject:_reschedule dinner?

Hi Yu, I'm really sorry, but we're going to have to reschedule the dinner we'd planned for this coming Saturday night. We were really looking forward to our visit – you're a genius on the BBQ! – but my boss just dumped a TON of work on me and it's going to take all weekend to get it finished. Please also apologize to Patricia and the kids, and maybe your bunch can come over here for dinner in a couple of weeks instead?

Chris

YOUR RESPONSE: Subject: _____

Answers on pg. 151

SECRET #77: LEAVING A VOICEMAIL – LISTENING & SPEAKING

Using the Situation pages (2 different pages, one for each partner) and one Message page each, the learners will work with a partner to practice leaving voicemails. They will pretend that the person that they want to speak to isn't home, so they have to leave a voicemail for him or her.

If no time is given, have the learners write down the time in your classroom.

EXAMPLE: Partner #1 has the following Situation:

Partner #1 is calling using the Situation page, and Partner #2 is pretending to be voicemail using the Message page. Then switch.

Situation: You want your friend and his/her family to come over to your place for dinner on Saturday night. Call them and invite them. Your number is 289-328-3090.

BRING! BRING! (sound of phone ringing)

Partner #2: *"Hello, this is _____ (my name). Sorry I'm not here to take your call, but if you leave your name & number, I'll get back to you as soon as I can. Thanks for calling!"*

Partner #1: *"Hello, this is _____ (my name). I would like to invite you and your family to come over for dinner on Saturday. Please call me back to let me know if you can come, thanks. My number is 289-328-3090. Talk to you soon!"*

PARTNER #2 will write the message on the Phone Message Pad

After the learners have taken turns giving and receiving messages, they can compare what their partner wrote down as a message to their own Situation card.

PHONE MESSAGE

FROM: ___Amir_____

TIME: ___10:10 a.m._____

MESSAGE: ___– go over to his place for___

_____dinner on Saturday night?_____

_____Call him to confirm._____

_____289-328-3090_____

Is the message right?

- OR -

If you want to use this lesson as a Listening Assessment, have the learners hand in the Message page for you to check.

PHOTOCOPIABLE BY PURCHASING TEACHER

SECRET #77: Leaving a Voicemail – PARTNER # 1 – Situations

In each situation, the person that you want to speak to isn't home, and you have to leave a voicemail for him or her. If no time is given, use the current time in your classroom.

(Don't show this page to your partner!)

Situation: You want to go out for dinner on Friday night. Call a friend or relative and invite him or her. Your number is 289-328-3090.

Situation: There is a film you want to see at a film festival downtown tomorrow night. Call your classmate and invite him or her (and his or her husband or wife) to come with you. Your number is 215-515-3452.

Situation: You are at the park. You and some friends want to play soccer, but don't have enough players. Call a friend and invite him/her to come to the park right now. Your number is 214-312-6651.

Situation: Call the doctor. Tell them your name, and that you had an appointment for tomorrow at 2 p.m., but you have to work, so you can't come. You'd like another appointment for the same time next week. Ask them to call you back to reschedule. Your number is 222-341-1689.

Situation: You are at school. The power has gone out, and you need someone to come and pick you up earlier than usual. Call your friend or to ask them to come and get you. Your number is 215-333-3949.

Situation: You are in your car. There has been a bad accident on the highway, and you are stuck in traffic, which isn't moving. Call someone at home to let them know you are okay and why you will be late getting home.

SECRET #77: Leaving Voicemail – PARTNER #2 – Situations

In each situation, the person that you want to speak to isn't home, and you have to leave a voicemail for him or her. If no time is given, use the current time in your classroom.

(Don't show this page to your partner!)

Situation: You are at home. You are sick, so you can't come to school today. Call your teacher to tell him or her that you won't be in school. Your number is 219-202-3945.	**Situation**: Call the dentist. Tell them your name, and that you had an appointment for tomorrow at 2 p.m., but you are sick, so you can't come. You'd like another appointment in 2 weeks. Ask them to call you back to reschedule. Your number is 222-909-1818.
Situation: You are at school. A classmate has invited you to go get a coffee before you go home. Call someone at home and tell them you will be a bit late in getting home. Tell them you will be home by 5 p.m.	**Situation**: Your child, _____ (name) is getting bullied at school. You want to make an appointment to speak to your child's teacher, Ms. Henshaw. Your number is 214-465-1122
Situation: You are at work. It's 5 p.m. Your shift will end in one hour, but someone has called in sick, and your boss has asked you to work 4 more hours. Call someone at home to tell them to come and get you at 10 p.m. instead of 6 p.m.	**Situation:** There is a great sale on at _____ (your favourite store). Call a friend and invite him or her to go shopping with you at this store. Your number is 217-555-1717.

SECRET #77: Leaving a Voicemail – Phone Message Pad

TAKE A MESSAGE. Pretend to be voicemail. When your partner calls, you must say, *"Hello, this is _____ (your name). Sorry I missed your call, but if you leave your name & number, I'll get back to you as soon as I can. Thanks for calling!"*
Write down their message on the pad below. When you've written all 6 messages, compare what you've written to your partner's original message. *How well did you do?*

PHONE MESSAGE	PHONE MESSAGE
FROM: _____ TIME: _____ MESSAGE: _____	FROM: _____ TIME: _____ MESSAGE: _____
PHONE MESSAGE	PHONE MESSAGE
FROM: _____ TIME: _____ MESSAGE: _____	FROM: _____ TIME: _____ MESSAGE: _____
PHONE MESSAGE	PHONE MESSAGE
FROM: _____ TIME: _____ MESSAGE: _____	FROM: _____ TIME: _____ MESSAGE: _____

SECRET #78: STARTING A BUSINESS – INTERNET RESEARCH

As a CLASS, BRAINSTORM 8 pieces of information you might need for starting a business. Divide into teams of 2-3. Each team will search for the address of ONE resource. When you're done, share your information with the rest of the class.

THING I NEED TO KNOW ABOUT STARTING A BUSINESS IN CANADA	RESOURCE (website or physical address NEAR YOU). Also provide contact phone number, dates & times & any costs, if possible.
1.	
2.	
3.	
4.	
5.	
6.	
7.	
8.	

Answers on pg.152

SECRET #79: THE HANDSHAKE CONTRACT – HOW LEGAL ARE YOUR CONTRACTS?

– SURVEY

Try to GUESS the answer for each country before you ask! Then survey your classmates, and fill in the following chart: If there is more than one person from a given country, check to see if they agree. If not, list the variations! Which country has the MOST INFORMAL ways of doing business? Which country uses WRITTEN contracts the MOST?

COUNTRY	Is a handshake contract legal?	How much business is conducted informally?	How much business is conducted with WRITTEN contracts?	How common are LEGAL DISPUTES in business?
Canada	YES	SMALL deals	LARGE deals	Not that common

SECRET #80: SMALL CLAIMS COURT: ROLE-PLAYING A COURT CASE

Divide the class into 2 teams – "Lawyers for the Home Owner" and "Lawyers for Big Promises Contracting". Give the teams 15-20 minutes to prepare their case, using the following details. Teams can make up any additional details that they want. Tell them to use their creativity – they want their client to WIN!

You can be the judge.

FACTS of the CASE:

- Bob and Mary decided to renovate their finished basement so that Mary's aging mother could move in.

- They wanted to create an "in-law" suite that they could rent out for additional income someday.

- They asked for an estimate to redo the flooring as well as add a kitchen and a full bathroom (with a bathtub/shower),

- They got estimates from 3 companies, who all promised it could be done in 2 weeks

a) Doowit Right Contracting = $35,000

b) Big Promises Contracting = $15,000

c) In The Middle Contracting = $25,000

- Being on a budget, Bob and Mary decided to go with Big Promises Contracting (BPC)

- They gave BPC all of the money up front ($15,000) with a handshake contract

- BPC showed up at 7 a.m. on Monday, Sept. 9th with a lead contractor, a carpenter, an electrician, and a plumber

- Bob and Mary both work full-time, so they left Mary's mother, Blanche, in charge

- For 3 days, everything seemed to be going well. The old flooring was torn up, and the bathroom and kitchen were "roughed in" – electricity and plumbing installed but not finished.

- Then, on Thursday, Sept. 12, nobody showed up. At noon, Blanche called Mary, who called BPC. There was no answer, so she left a voicemail.

- BPC never came back.

- After repeated attempts to get the company to complete the project, Bob and Mary are suing BPC for $10,000 – the labour cost to finish the basement

- BPC is arguing that they told the couple that the $15,000 was for materials costs alone and that Bob and Mary agreed to pay them an additional $15,000 for labour

- BPC says that unless Bob and Mary pay $15,000 more, the project will not be completed

SECRET #81: EQUAL PAY FOR EQUAL WORK? – ATTITUDES SURVEY

Work with partners from 2 other countries. Try to GUESS TRUE or FALSE about your partners' cultures and for CANADA. After everyone has guessed, discuss the results.

CHALLENGE:	PARTNER'S Name: COUNTRY:	PARTNER'S Name: COUNTRY:	COUNTRY: CANADA
1. Men earn more than women in general.			
2. Men and women who do the same job earn the same pay.			
3. Men do jobs that women can't do.			
4. "Women's work" – such as childcare – isn't as valuable to the economy.			
5. Women get promoted as often as men.			
6. There aren't many female CEOs.			
7. Women don't want to run companies.			
8. Women are too emotional to make tough business decisions.			
9. Other? (Your idea)			

Answers on pg. 153

SECRET #82: ATTITUDES TOWARD THE POLICE – CONVERSATION

In small groups, discuss the differences between the roles of police officers and how people feel about them in different countries, using the following questions to get you started.

1. Are police officers civil or military in your country of birth?

2. Are most police officers trustworthy in your country of birth?

3. How do people generally feel about the police?

4. Are police officers well paid?

5. Are police officers part of your SECRET Police?

6. Are police officers generally respectful?

7. Are police officers usually violent?

8. If you get arrested in your country of birth, do you think your human rights will be respected?

9. Are police officers mostly male or what percent are female?

10. Would a female police officer deal with a female prisoner?

11. Do you think police officers in your country of birth are protecting the public or serving the rich?

12. Do you know anyone who has dealt with the police in your country of birth? What happened?

13. Would you trust a police officer in Canada?

14. Why do you think that most of our police officers are honest?

15. Do you think that the police in Canada are racist? Why or why not?

16. Do you think that the police in Canada treat men and women equally? If not, what might the differences be?

SECRET #83: WHAT ARE OUR HUMAN RIGHTS? – BRAINSTORMING

The United Nations has issued a <u>Universal Declaration of Human Rights</u>.

Try to come up with the 30 rights.

1.	16.
2.	17.
3.	18.
4.	19.
5.	20.
6.	21.
7.	22.
8.	23.
9.	24.
10.	25.
11.	26.
12.	27.
13.	28.
14.	29.
15.	30.

Answers on pg. 154-155

SECRET #84: RECOGNIZING ABUSE – BRAINSTORMING

Which of the following actions may be considered ABUSIVE in Canada?

Write <u>Yes</u>, <u>No</u> or <u>Maybe</u> beside each one.

1. Throwing something at you such as a phone, book, shoe or plate _____

2. Extramarital affairs _____

3. Humiliating or embarrassing you repeatedly _____

4. Pushing or pulling you _____

5. Isolating you from friends and family _____

6. Grabbing your clothing but not your body _____

7. Controlling the household money alone _____

8. Sending you text messages, voicemails, videos, letters, photos and gifts after you have asked them to stop _____

9. Unreasonable jealousy _____

10. Smacking your bottom without your permission or consent _____

11. Forcing you to have sex or perform a sexual act _____

12. Making everything your fault _____

13. Allowing other people (e.g., mother-in-law) to control or yell at you _____

14. Grabbing your face to make you look at them _____

15. Grabbing you to prevent you from leaving or to force you to go somewhere _____

16. Threatening to commit suicide if you leave _____

17. Denying you the right to be alone or spend time with friends and family without your partner

_____

18. Constantly calling or texting when you are not with him/her _____

19. Demanding that you share your banking or internet passwords _____

20. Making fun of you _____

21. Yelling at you until you cry _____

22. Threatening you by raising a hand as if to hit you _____

Answers on pg. 156

Try to GUESS the answer for each country before you ask! Then survey your classmates, and fill in the following chart: If there is more than one person from a given country, check to see if they agree. If not, list the variations!

COUNTRY?	There is no age limit for children to be home alone.	If there is a limit, what age is it?	Is it common for kids to stay home alone for hours?	If you are caught leaving your kids alone at home, they can be taken away from you.
Canada	NO	12-16	12 & up, YES ("latchkey kids")	YES

SECRET #86: STAYING IN SCHOOL – CONVERSATION

In small groups, discuss some of the following questions:

1. In your country of birth, is there a minimum age you that must be before you can leave school permanently (drop out)?

   - If so, what is it?

2. How common is it for kids to drop out before finishing high school?

3. Why do you think this is? Why do some kids drop out of school?

4. Do you know what the average amount of education is across the population of your country of birth? (If not, see if you can Google it.)

5. Did your parents graduate from high school?

   - If no, what jobs did they have?

6. Did your grandparents graduate from high school?

   - If no, what jobs did they have?

7. Did your parents graduate from university or college?

   - If yes, what job(s) did they have?

8. Did your grandparents graduate from university or college?

   - If yes, what job(s) did they have?

9. Do you think your kids will graduate (or have they already graduated) from college or university?

   - If yes, what job(s) do you think they will have / do they have?

   - If no, what job(s) do you think they will have / do they have?

SECRET #87: WHEN ARE YOU A LEGAL ADULT? AGE OF MAJORITY – SURVEY

Work with partners from 2 other countries. Try to GUESS <u>TRUE</u> or <u>FALSE</u> about your partners' cultures and for CANADA. After everyone has guessed, discuss the results.

	PARTNER'S Name:	PARTNER'S Name:	
CHALLENGE:	COUNTRY:	COUNTRY:	COUNTRY: **CANADA**
1. You are a legal adult at 18 years old.			
2. You are a legal adult at 21 years old.			
3. You can't own property until you're a legal adult.			
4. You can't vote until you're a legal adult.			
5. You can drive a car at 16 years old.			
6. You can drink alcohol legally at 18.			
7. You can get married at any age (with parent's permission)			
8. You can start working legally at any age.			
10. Other? (Your idea)			

Answers on pg. 157

SECRET #88: PERMANENT RESIDENT or CANADIAN CITIZEN? – CONVERSATION

It's possible to live your whole life quite comfortably in Canada without ever becoming a citizen.

In small groups, discuss why some people choose to remain a Permanent Resident (PR), and why others choose to become Canadian citizens.

1. Give 5 reasons why people might choose to remain a Permanent Resident in Canada.

   a. _____

   b. _____

   c. _____

   d. _____

   e. _____

2. Give 5 reasons why people might choose to become a Canadian citizen.

   a. _____

   b. _____

   c. _____

   d. _____

   e. _____

3. Do you think any group or nationality is less likely to choose to become citizens? Who is this, and why?

4. Do you think your age when you come to Canada affects your decision whether or not to become a citizen? How so?

5. Do you think it's important to become a citizen so that you have the right to vote?

6. What does it mean if you can never vote in Canada?

7. What effect does it have if your children are Canadian citizens, but you are not?

8. Does it matter if your grandchildren are Canadian citizens, but you are not?

SECRET #89: ATTITUDE TOWARD PETS – CONVERSATION

In small groups, discuss how people feel about pets in different countries, using the following questions to get you started.

1. Is it common for people to have a dog in your country of birth?

   • If yes, are the dogs generally kept indoors or outdoors?

   • If not, why do you think people don't have dogs?

2. Are dogs used for work (shepherding or guarding domestic animals such as sheep or goats, for police work, border security, etc.) in your country of birth?

3. Is it common for people to have a cat in your country of birth?

   • If not, why do you think people don't have cats?

4. What are some other common pets in your country of birth?

5. "Exotic pets" (such as cheetahs and tigers) are illegal in most parts of Canada. Are they legal in your country of birth?

   • If yes, how common is it for people to have an exotic pet?

   • If not, what is the penalty for keeping such an animal?

   • Which people are most likely to own such an animal?

   • Do you think it's okay to keep these kinds of animals in captivity?

6. Is it expensive to keep a pet in your country of birth?

7. Most Canadians feel that taking care of a pet is a good way for an older child (12+) to learn to accept responsibility. Do you agree?

SECRET #90: BENEFITS OF SPIRITUAL BELIEFS – BRAINSTORMING & SURVEY

As a CLASS, BRAINSTORM 8 possible benefits (physical, psychological, social) that religious or spiritual beliefs may have. (Research at the Mayo Clinic **in the U.S. has proven that there ARE real benefits.) Then break into small groups and DISCUSS if you believe these to be <u>TRUE</u> for you or your partners.**

SOME POSSIBLE BENEFITS OF SPIRITUAL BELIEFS	PARTNER'S Name: COUNTRY:	PARTNER'S Name: COUNTRY:	PARTNER'S Name: COUNTRY:
1.			
2.			
3.			
4.			
5.			
6.			
7.			
8.			

SECRET #91: COMPLAINING EFFECTIVELY – MATCHING & CONVERSATION

Match the complaints on the left with the appropriate ending on the right.

COMPLAINT – BEGINNING		COMPLAINT – ENDING
1. You **can't** …		A. … some editing.
2. I **wish** you **wouldn't** …		B. … high taxes.
3. My boss is **always griping about** …		C. … work overtime for no pay.
4. Your report **could use /could do with** …		D. … eat that entire pizza yourself!
5. I **wish** my students **would** ...		E. … this shoddy workmanship.
6. The citizens **are protesting** …		F. … bark all night.
7. I **refuse to** …		G. … the poor service you've given us.
8. Our customers **won't accept** …		H. … smoke on your balcony. The smoke always blows in my windows.
9. Her dog **tends to** …		I. … complete their homework all the time.
10. I'd like to **speak to your manager about** …		J. … paying us overtime.

How do you complain in the following situations?

- My office is always cold.
- My pay is wrong.
- My co-worker keeps making sexist remarks.
- My co-worker keeps making racist remarks.
- The fridge at work is always stinky.
- My co-worker has bad breath or B.O. (Body Odour).
- The clients keep calling me, when they should be speaking to my team leader.
- I have a designated parking space, but somebody else keeps parking there.
- My co-worker keeps criticizing my work even though he's my equal.
- Someone always smokes just outside the door that I use to enter the building.
- My neighbour's children are always riding their bikes in my driveway.

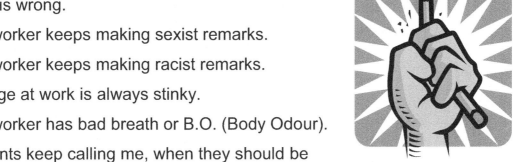

Answers on pg. 158-159

PHOTOCOPIABLE BY PURCHASING TEACHER

SECRET #92: The BAD NEWS SANDWICH – REWRITING EMAILS

With your partner, look at the following emails and REWRITE the "bad news" in a more positive way, using the "bad news sandwich" approach.

ONLY rewrite the CONTENT of each email.

#1. **To:** badbob@ABCstuff.ca
From: supervisor@ABCstuff.ca
Subject: Tardiness

Bob, you have arrived late 3 times this month. If you don't shape up, you're going to get FIRED.
U.R. Intrable, Manager

Your REWRITE:

#2. **To:** badparents@gmail.com
From: goodteacher@bestschool.ca
Subject: Erica's failing

Dear Mr. and Mrs. Badparents,
This is to inform you that your daughter Erica is failing Grade 1 and will probably have to repeat her year.
Ms. Goodteacher

Your REWRITE:

Answers on pg. 160

SECRET #93: THINKING ABOUT EQUALITY – CONVERSATION

In small groups, discuss the following questions. Find out if there is a cultural element to them, or if it varies more between individuals. Do people from the same country of birth or region always AGREE?

1. What do you think of when you hear the word 'equality'?

2. Do you think true equality is actually possible? If not, why not?

3. What factors affect our status as equal or unequal?

4. In your own experience, where do you think you experienced equality the best? (At school, at work, with friends or family?)

5. In your own experience, where do you think you experienced equality the LEAST?

6. Do your friends tend to treat you as their equal?

• If not, who is seen as the superior and who is the inferior, and why?

7. If there were two or more children in your family, did your parents treat all of the children in your family as equals?

8. Did you belong to an oppressed group at school, at work, or socially?

9. Do you know anyone who has belonged to an oppressed group?

10. Do you think you have more equality in a democracy?

11. Do you try to treat your children as equals?

12. How can we foster equality:

   – at home?

   – at work?

   – in our society?

SECRET #94: THINKING ABOUT RACISM – CONVERSATION

Watch the following 3 commercials on YouTube:

- **The New Sauvage Dior Film Starring Johnny Depp 2019**
- **Racism in a Chinese laundry detergent advertisement**
- **Get Happy | Volkswagen Super Bowl 2013 spot**

NOW, in small groups, discuss what's WRONG with them by answering these questions:

1. What racial stereotype(s) does each one show?

   a. _____

   b. _____

   c. _____

2. What IMAGE for their PRODUCT did the advertising companies responsible for these commercial want to portray?

   a. _____

   b. _____

   c. _____

3. Two of these ads (b. & c.) were intended to be FUNNY. - Are they?

4. Some people would argue that these ads are "harmless". Do you agree?

5. Who would laugh at these ads?

6. How do these ads DAMAGE our view of these races?

Now watch THIS commercial on YouTube:

Nike what are girls made of

7. How is this commercial different from the first 3?

8. Does it make you want to buy their product? (- women in the class? - men in the class?)

SECRET #95: THINKING ABOUT SEXISM – BRAINSTORMING

What do you think are the major warning signs for a heart attack in MEN?

1. _____

2. _____

3. _____

4. _____

5. _____

6. _____

Watch this Public Service commercial on YouTube:

Elizabeth Banks in "Just a Little Heart Attack"

What do you think are the major warning signs for a heart attack in WOMEN?

1. _____

2. _____

3. _____

4. _____

5. _____

6. _____

Google: The #RedList to learn more about heart disease research on women in Canada

Women are not small men
Not researching the difference is proving fatal for women.

Answers on pg. 161

SECRET #96: THINKING ABOUT AGEISM – CONVERSATION

In small groups, discuss the following questions. Find out if there is a cultural element to them, or if it varies more between individuals. Do people from the same country of birth or region always AGREE?

1. Are seniors well treated in your country of birth?

2. Do you have a mandatory retirement age? If so, what is it?

3. If not, how long do people typically keep working?

4. Is it different for women than for men?

5. After you retire, do you get a government pension?

   - If so, is it enough to live on?

6. After you retire, do most people get a company pension?

   - If so, is it enough to live on?

7. If you don't get enough pension funds to be able to live comfortably, do seniors go back to work?

8. Where can they work?

9. Is there prejudice against older workers?

10. Do seniors start businesses?

11. Is there prejudice against a business started by a senior?

12. Do most people expect their children to support them financially in their retirement?

    - If so, do the children really support them financially?

13. Are you saving for your retirement?

14. Do you know how to save for retirement in Canada? (learn about RRSPs)

SECRET #97: SOCIAL CLASSES – MONEY OR RESPECT? – BRAINSTORMING & SURVEY

In small groups, BRAINSTORM which jobs are the TOP 10 BEST PAID jobs in your country of birth as well as in Canada. (Look up the ANSWERS on the Internet if you can.)

Then BRAINSTORM which jobs you think are the TOP 10 MOST RESPECTED jobs in your country of birth as well as in Canada.

	PARTNER'S Name:	PARTNER'S Name:	
TOP 10 BEST PAID JOBS	COUNTRY:	COUNTRY:	COUNTRY: CANADA
1.			
2.			
3.			
4.			
5.			
6.			
7.			
8.			
9.			
10.			
TOP 10 MOST RESPECTED JOBS			
1.			
2.			
3.			
4.			
5.			
6.			
7.			
8.			
9.			
10.			

Answers on pg. 162

SECRET #98: OUR SHAMEFUL TREATMENT OF INDIGENOUS PEOPLES –

CANADA'S APOLOGY FOR RESIDENTIAL SCHOOLS

On June 11, 2008, former Prime Minister Stephen Harper offered a full apology on behalf of Canadians for the Indian Residential Schools system in the House of Commons. This is a portion of the apology. Read Canada's apology and discuss.

I stand before you, in this Chamber so central to our life as a country, to apologize to Aboriginal peoples for Canada's role in the Indian Residential Schools system.

To the approximately 80,000 living former students, and all family members and communities, the Government of Canada now recognizes that it was wrong to forcibly remove children from their homes and we apologize for having done this.

We now recognize that it was wrong to separate children from rich and vibrant cultures and traditions that it created a void in many lives and communities, and we apologize for having done this.

We now recognize that, in separating children from their families, we undermined the ability of many to adequately parent their own children and sowed the seeds for generations to follow, and we apologize for having done this.

We now recognize that, far too often, these institutions gave rise to abuse or neglect and were inadequately controlled, and we apologize for failing to protect you.

Not only did you suffer these abuses as children, but as you became parents, you were powerless to protect your own children from suffering the same experience, and for this we are sorry.

The burden of this experience has been on your shoulders for far too long. The burden is properly ours as a Government, and as a country. There is no place in Canada for the attitudes that inspired the Indian Residential Schools system to ever prevail again.

You have been working on recovering from this experience for a long time and in a very real sense, we are now joining you on this journey.

The Government of Canada sincerely apologizes and asks the forgiveness of the Aboriginal peoples of this country for failing them so profoundly.

> Nous le regrettons
>
> We are sorry
>
> Nimitataynan
>
> Niminchinowesamin
>
> Mamiattugut

The Right Honourable Stephen Harper,

Prime Minister of Canada

**For more (simple English) resources on this topic,
Google: Grade 5 Indian Residential Schools and Reconciliation**

SECRET #99: FRENCH vs. BRITISH – COLONIALISM IN CANADA – CONVERSATION

Look at the 2 maps below, showing North America in 1750 & 1803. Discuss how much Canada changed in just 53 years!

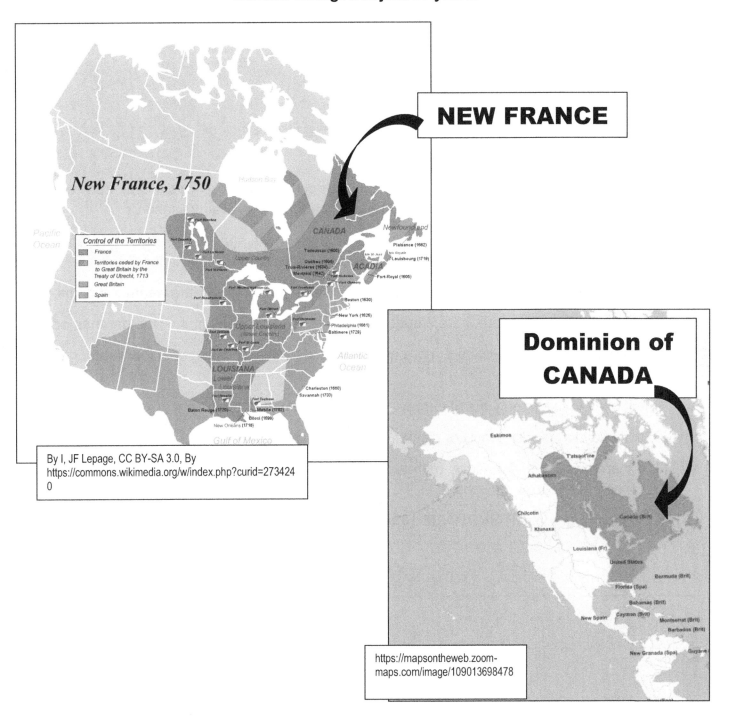

By I, JF Lepage, CC BY-SA 3.0, By https://commons.wikimedia.org/w/index.php?curid=2734240

https://mapsontheweb.zoom-maps.com/image/109013698478

Has there been a period of time when your country of birth went through a similar period of colonization and re-colonization?

Tell your group about it!

SECRET #100: SEASONAL AFFECTIVE DISORDER (S.A.D.) – CONVERSATION

In small groups, discuss some of the following questions.

1. What are some different moods that people can be in?

2. Name 8 things that can affect a person's mood.

3. What puts you in a good mood?

4. What puts you in a bad mood?

5. Do overcast skies or rainy weather make you sad?

6. If not, how do they make you feel?

7. Are people affected by different seasons in your country of birth? (Even if you don't have winter, people's moods can also be negatively affected by a rainy season.)

8. Are your moods different in different seasons? If so, which season is best for you, and which is worst. Tell us why (if you're comfortable sharing this information).

9. Do you think women are more emotionally sensitive to changes in the weather than men?

10. Do you think children are more emotionally sensitive to changes in the weather than adults?

11. Do you think older people are more emotionally sensitive to changes in the weather than younger people?

12. Is it okay to talk openly about depression in your country of birth?

13. Is it okay to talk with family or close friends about depression?

14. Is there anyone in your family (parents, siblings, children, etc.) who gets "sad" in some seasons? How do they cope?

15. With your group, **BRAINSTORM 10 things you can do to cope** with winter in Canada:

SECRET #101: YOU CAN HAVE A GOOD LIFE IN CANADA – SUMMING UP –

In a small group, BRAINSTORM the

TOP 10 SECRETS OF SUCCESS IN CANADA:

1.
2.
3.
4.
5.
6.
7.
8.
9.
10.

When you're done, compare your list to that of other groups, and as a CLASS, come up with what you agree are the –

TOP TOP-10 SECRETS OF SUCCESS IN CANADA:

1.
2.
3.
4.
5.
6.
7.
8.
9.
10.

WHERE TO LEARN MORE ABOUT CANADA:

Here are some ways to learn more about Canadian Culture:

BOOK: Always My Child: A Parent's Guide to Understanding Your Gay, Lesbian, Bisexual, Transgendered, or Questioning Son or Daughter

GOOGLE:

- settlement.org ★ (LOTS of GREAT info!)

- meetup.com (put in your Postal Code)

- Telehealth Ontario

- Canada Child Support Calculator

- Finding a job – Canada.ca

- What is Enhanced Language Training

- Toastmasters

- Starting a business - Canada.ca

- Raptor's Super Fan

- Child Welfare Services

- social register in communications in Canada

- Age of Majority in Canada

- Canadian Human Rights Code

- Women's shelter _____ (your city)

- wix.com (free websites)

- vistaprint.ca (low-cost business cards)

ANSWERS:

WARMUP: WHAT DO YOU ALREADY KNOW ABOUT CANADA? – QUIZ
ANSWERS:

1. 75% of Canadians speak English as their mother tongue — **FALSE. About 50%**

2. Chinese (Mandarin) is the 3rd most common language in Canada — **TRUE**

3. Canadians don't say, "How are you?" every time they meet — **TRUE**

4. You should stand an arm's length away from a Canadian when you talk — **TRUE**

5. Canadians are very emotional in public — **FALSE**

6. Canadians are reserved with strangers, but friendly if you get to know them — **TRUE**

7. Canadians usually initiate friendships with their new neighbours — **FALSE**

8. If you're invited to dinner, you can always bring your kids — **FALSE**

9. You should BYOB (Bring Your Own Beverage) to a party — **TRUE**

10. Canadians usually live together before they get married — **TRUE**

11. Men and women share housework equally — **FALSE**

12. The parents of the bride usually pay for the wedding — **FALSE**

13. After a divorce, most Canadians share custody of the kids — **FALSE**

14. Employers in Canada consider volunteer work almost equal to paid work — **TRUE**

15. All Canadians earn equal pay for equal work — **FALSE**

16. Being late for work can get you fired — **TRUE**

17. Canadians socialize with their boss — **FALSE**

18. A handshake contract is legal in Canada — **TRUE**

19. The police in Canada are mostly honest — **TRUE**

20. Kids can stay home alone after 12 years old — **FALSE**

21. Canadians are indirect when delivering bad news — **TRUE**

22. Canada doesn't have social classes — **FALSE**

PHOTOCOPIABLE BY PURCHASING TEACHER

SECRET #2: COURTESY: EVERYDAY RESPONSES – SOME POSSIBLE ANSWERS:

WHEN SOMEONE SAYS …	WHAT SHOULD YOU SAY?
Why did you come to Canada? (this is very personal & may be rude to ask)	I'd rather not say. / Can I tell you another time? **RUDE:** None of your business.
Can I bring a friend to your party?	Sure! The more the merrier! / I'm sorry; I can only accommodate 10 people. Maybe next time?
I just graduated from university.	Congratulations! / Good for you! / That's great!
How much do I owe you for dinner?	Nothing. It's my treat! / It's on me!
My son Timmy's in trouble at school again.	I'm sorry to hear that. / He must take after his father.
Would you like a diet Coke?	That would be lovely, thanks. / Sure! / No, thanks, I'm good. / Just water, please.
They didn't hire me.	Better luck next time. / I'm sorry to hear that. / Jerks! (only with close friends/family)
What's Rick's last name?	I'm sorry, I don't know. Maybe you could ask _____ (name someone else). / I'm not sure. / Sorry, I don't know.
Will you lend me $1,000,000?	I wish I could. / You must be kidding!
Can I borrow some paper?	Sure! Help yourself! / Sorry, I don't have any extra.
I'll buy the drinks.	Okay, I'll get the next round. / Let's split the check. / No, thanks, I can get my own.
May I use your phone?	Sure, here you go. / Sorry, it's not charged.
Can I smoke in your house / car?	Sure, no problem. / Sorry, I'd rather you didn't. Can you go outside to smoke?
I hope I get the job.	I'll keep my fingers crossed for you. / They'll be lucky to have you!
Can I date your sister?	It's up to her. Give me your number & I'll pass it on. / In your dreams! (not polite)
My grandfather passed away.	I'm very sorry to hear that. / My condolences.
Can I come too?	Sure! The more the merrier! / Sorry, maybe next time.

SECRET #9: TABOOS – POSSIBLE ANSWERS

QUESTION	YOUR COUNTRY OF BIRTH	IN CANADA
"Do you buy lottery tickets?"		2 (okay for close friends)
"Do you like wine?"		0
"Do you like to gamble?"		4
"Do you have any allergies?"		0
"Do you have any illnesses?"		5
"Do you have any painkillers with you?"		1
"Do you cheat on your spouse?"		5
"Do you prefer a bath or a shower?"		4 (Okay for close female friends)
"Do you see fortune tellers?"		2 (okay for close friends)
"Do you wear glasses?"		0
"Do you wear pajamas to sleep?"		4 (Okay for close female friends)
"What do you think of abortion?"		5
"What do you think about euthanasia?"		4
"How do you feel about your mother-in-law?"		3
"How long do you spend exercising every week?"		2
"How many pairs of shoes do you have?"		1
"How much do you weigh?"		5
"How much money do you earn?"		5
"How much money do you spend on going out?"		5
"How often do you get drunk?"		5
"How often do you take a bath or shower?"		5
"How often do you tidy up your house or apartment?"		4
"What do you think about nuclear power?"		3
"Where do you buy underwear?"		4 (Okay for close female friends)
"Where do you come from?"		0
"Where do you usually go on holiday?"		0

SECRET #10: PERSONAL QUESTIONS – SOME *POSSIBLE* ANSWERS:

Information Questions: "Excuse me …	Beginning of noun clause "Excuse me …	Question Word	Subject	Verb
Where is the post office?	Could you please tell me	where	the post office	is?
When is the next bus coming?	Do you happen to know	when	the next bus	is coming?
Who is that man over there?	Do you know	who	that man over there	is?
How much does this _____ cost?	Can you please tell me	how much	this _____	costs?
Where is Claire?	Do you happen to know	where	Claire	is?
How old are you?	Do you mind if I ask		your age?	
Where is the washroom?	Could you please tell me	where	the washroom	is?
Why did ____ go home?	Do you happen to know	why	_____	went home?
When is the summer break?	Can you please tell me	when	the summer break	is?
Who is the manager or owner?	Do you mind telling me	who	the owner	is?
What time is it?	Do you happen to know		the time?	
When will you be finished?	Do you mind if I ask	when	you	will be finished?
Where were you last night?	Could you please tell me	where	you	were last night?
What do you want?	Can I help you?			
How much did you pay for your house?	Do you mind if I ask	how much	you	paid for your house?

SECRET #11: TONE – EXPRESSING EMOTIONS
Some POSSIBLE ANSWERS:

1.	Boy, you're something, do you know that? You are really something!	**Anger**
2.	Oh, man. I don't want to do this – I really don't.	**Reluctance**
3.	I can't believe it! It was the most exciting thing that's ever happened!	**Excitement**
4.	It was so funny! You had to be there – it was a classic!	**Humour**
5.	Oh, I wish I could go. I'd give anything if I could be there.	**Sadness**
6.	I don't want to talk about it. In fact, I don't even want to think about it.	**Anger**
7.	I really like you. You're easy to talk to, you know?	**Flirtation / Interest**
8.	Look, it's none of your business. Okay? Just leave me alone.	**Anger**
9.	I wish that things were like they used to be. It was a lot easier back then.	**Sadness**
10.	What did you do that for? What's wrong with you?	**Anger**
11.	God! / Gosh! I'm so nervous. I just can't seem to calm down.	**Anxiety**
12.	Oh God! / Gosh! It hurts! Can't you do something about it?	**Pain**
13.	I don't care. I really don't care at this point.	**Frustration**
14.	Something's wrong, isn't it? You're afraid to tell me, is that it?	**Worried**
15.	Did you really? Go on – you're kidding me!	**Excitement / Interest**
16.	I'm not sure I understand. Tell me again; I'm just not sure what you mean.	**Confusion**
17.	Where have you been? Do you know how long I've been waiting for you?	**Anger**
18.	I hope they're all right. I just hope nothing's happened.	**Worried**
19.	Hey, everything's Great. Things couldn't be better:	**Excitement (high tone) / Sarcasm (flat tone)**
20.	Well . . . I mean . . . Okay Okay. Let me start again.	**Anxiety**

SECRET #14: PUBLIC DISPLAYS OF EMOTIONS
Some *POSSIBLE* ANSWERS: (May vary strongly between individuals & families)

QUESTION	YOUR COUNTRY OF BIRTH	IN CANADA
1. Is it okay to cry in public?		**NO**
2. Is it okay to cry in front of your family?		**YES**
3. Is it okay to yell at members of your family?		**NO**
4. Is it okay to yell at your spouse?		**NO** (but we DO)
5. Is it okay to yell at your child?		**NO** (but we DO)
6. Is it okay to yell at your parent(s)?		**NO**
7. Is it okay to yell at a neighbour?		**NO**
8. Is it okay to yell at a person at work?		**NO**
9. Is it okay to yell at someone on the street?		**NO**
10. Is it okay to yell at a server in a restaurant?		**NO**
11. Is it okay to argue loudly in a restaurant? (debating)		**NO**
12. Is it okay to argue loudly at work? (debating)		**NO**
13. Is it okay to argue loudly at a friend's? (debating)		**YES**? (depends)
14. Is it okay to argue loudly on the bus? (debating)		**NO**
15. Is it okay to argue loudly at home? (debating)		**YES**? (depends)
16. Is there a difference in these rules between men and women?		**YES** – but it's *changing*
a. Who can cry? (men and/or women)		**women** (in the past)
b. Who can yell? (men and/or women)		**men** (in the past)
c. Who can argue loudly? (men and/or women)		**men** (in the past)
17. Is there a difference between social classes?		**YES** (showing emotion is lower class)

SECRET #15: RESTAURANT ETIQUETTE: BRAINSTORMING
Some POSSIBLE ANSWERS – or this dialogue could be used for a ROLE-PLAY activity!

HOST: "Welcome to Chez Nous. This will be your table. Your server will be right with you.

CUSTOMER: "<u>Oh, I'm sorry, but I'd rather not</u> sit by the kitchen. <u>Is another table available?</u>"
       1   **2**

HOST: "I'm sorry, sir. Follow me, and I'll take you to a different one."

CUSTOMER: "<u>Thank you very much</u>."
       3

HOST: "Is this table acceptable?"

CUSTOMER: "<u>Yes, thanks</u>."
       4

HOST: "Your server will be right with you. His name is Gaston."

SERVER: "Good evening. My name is Gaston. I'll be your server for tonight."

CUSTOMER: "<u>Hello, Gaston ... That's an interesting name</u>."
       5   **6**

SERVER: "It's a French name. I'm originally from France."

CUSTOMER: "<u>Really? How are you liking Canada? ... Would it be possible to get a whiskey sour? I've had a rough day</u>."   **7**   **8**

SERVER: "Of course, sir. Right away." (Brings the drink and the Menu)

CUSTOMER: "Okay." (Looks at the menu.) "What <u>do you recommend</u>?"
                                       9

SERVER: "Our Plat du Jour is filet mignon with grilled asparagus, for $39.99"

CUSTOMER: "<u>That sounds perfect</u>."
       10

SERVER: "How would you like your steak, sir?"

CUSTOMER: "Rare, <u>please</u>."
       11

SERVER: "Very good, sir. Would you like another whiskey while you wait?"

SECRET #17: TIPPING – LET'S DO SOME MATH!
SOME POSSIBLE ANSWERS:

SITUATION	TOTAL	APPROPRIATE TIP in CANADA
1. Family Restaurant	$50	$9 - $10
2. Expensive Restaurant	$400	$80 - $90
3. Bar	$8	$2
4. MacDonald's	$18	$2
5. Tim Hortons	$2	$0.25
6. Food Delivery	$30	$5
7. Haircut (women)	$40	$6 - $8
8. Haircut (men)	$25	$3
9. Taxi ride	$17	$3 - $5
10. Room Service	$110	$17 - $22
EXAMPLES FROM YOUR COUNTRY OF BIRTH	AVERAGE TOTAL	TIP?
11. Restaurant		
12. Bar		
13. Coffee Shop		
14. Haircut		
15. Taxi		

SECRET #20: HOCKEY POSITIONS – ANSWERS:

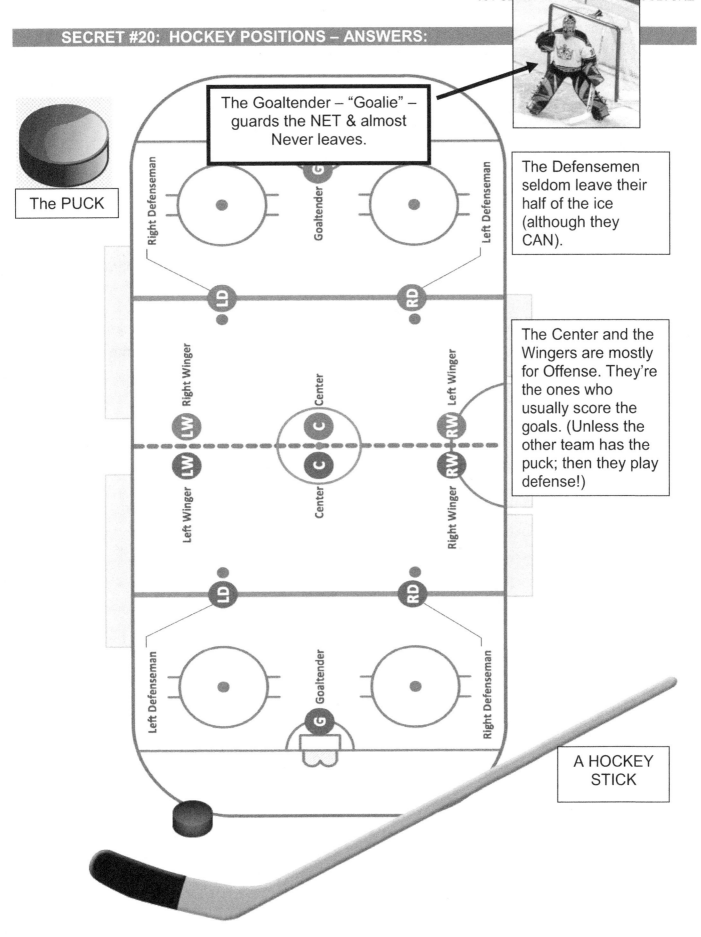

The PUCK

The Goaltender – "Goalie" – guards the NET & almost Never leaves.

The Defensemen seldom leave their half of the ice (although they CAN).

The Center and the Wingers are mostly for Offense. They're the ones who usually score the goals. (Unless the other team has the puck; then they play defense!)

A HOCKEY STICK

SECRET #25: WHO CAN YOU SOCIALIZE WITH AT WORK?
Some *POSSIBLE* ANSWERS for CANADA:

	PARTNER'S Name:	PARTNER'S Name:	
CHALLENGE:	**COUNTRY:**	**COUNTRY:**	COUNTRY: **CANADA**
1. It's normal to socialize with your boss or supervisor after work.			No
2. It's okay to chat with co-workers during work hours.			No (only coffee break, lunchtime & after work)
3. You can socialize with any co-workers after work.			No (Varies by company. Some companies prohibit "fraternizing".)
4. It's common to invite your boss to your house for dinner.			No (Used to be true; may still be true in some companies.)
5. It's important to be friends with the 'RIGHT' people (office POLITICS).			YES. There IS such a thing as "office politics". Google it!
6. It's normal to use office friendships to advance your career.			YES. (Nobody admits it, but being friends with the "right" people MAY advance your career.)
7. It's okay to go out with your colleagues for a drink (alcohol) at lunchtime.			No. (But it may be normal with clients.) Smelling of alcohol can get you FIRED.
8. Male and female co-workers can be friends.			Yes …? Friendships between men & women are becoming more common but may result in office GOSSIP.

SECRET #28: POLITE LANGUAGE for INVITING, ACCEPTING, REFUSING, & being UNCERTAIN

Formal Invitations: Use these the *first time you invite someone*, or when speaking to an *older person*, or for *formal* or organized events such as *birthdays, anniversaries, retirements* and *other celebrations*. Could be *verbal* or *in writing*.	**Formal Ways to:** **Accept, Refuse, Express Uncertainty**
Would you like to …	Sure! I'd love to. Thanks!
We are having a … party on Dec. 20th. Would you like to come?	Sorry, I'd like to, but I already have plans for that day.
Would you and your family like to come over for dinner this Saturday?	Um, could I let you know? I might have to work. I'm on call.
DATING: Hi, _____. I was wondering if you'd like to go out for a coffee sometime.	*DATING:* Sure! How about on Saturday? / Oh, sorry, I already have a boyfriend/husband etc.
Informal Invitations: Use these with family & people you know well. Could be *verbal* or *in an email/text*.	**Informal Ways to Accept, Refuse, Express Uncertainty**
My friends and I are going to a movie this coming Saturday evening. Wanna come?	Sure! That sounds great! Thanks!
Wanna play tennis this Saturday?	Sorry, I can't. I already have plans for that day. Rain check?
Can you and your family come out with us this Saturday? We're going to the Mandarin.	Um, I'll have to check with my husband/wife and let you know, okay?
Are you doing anything tonight?* *(This *sounds like* a *casual information question*, but is *often* an *invitation* – if you're free, the invitation will follow.)	Um, can I let you know? I might have to work. I'm on call.
Casual Invitations: Used only with your closest friends & family members. *Not used with people older than you.*	**Casual Ways to Accept, Refuse, Express Uncertainty**
Wanna grab a coffee after class?	Absolutely! Let's go!
Doing anything tonight?	Sorry, yeah, gotta work. How about tomorrow?
Come over for dinner on Saturday, ok?	Depends … whatcha cooking? ;)

SECRET #30: PUNCTUALITY – HOW IMPORTANT IS IT TO BE ON TIME?
Some _POSSIBLE_ ANSWERS:

HOW IMPORTANT IS IT TO BE ON TIME? RATE the following according to this scale:

Type of Appointment	Scheduled Time	PARTNER 1 NAME:	PARTNER 2 NAME:	CANADA
Starting Work (_hourly_ work)	9 A.M.			3 ("on time" means 10-15 min EARLY!)
Starting Work (_salaried_ work)	9 A.M.			2 (may work Flex Time)
Dentist or Doctor	10:15 A.M.			3 ("on time" means 10-15 min EARLY!)
Doctor (_Specialist_)	10:15 A.M.			3 ("on time" means 10-15 min EARLY!)
School	9 A.M.			3 ("on time" means 10-15 min EARLY!)
Lunch with a friend at _home_	12 P.M.			1-2 (not more than 15 minutes late)
Lunch with a friend at a _restaurant_	12 P.M.			2 (not more than 15 minutes late)
Arriving home for dinner with your family	6 P.M.			1-3 (varies between families)
Making dinner for your family (time to finish)	6 P.M.			1-3 (varies between families)
A friend's party	8 P.M.			2 (not more than 30 minutes late)
A work party	8 P.M.			2 (not more than 15 minutes late)
A performance review	9 A.M.			3 ("on time" means 10-15 min EARLY!)
A job interview	2 P.M.			3 ("on time" means 10-15 min EARLY!)

SECRET #33: Dress Codes – BRAINSTORM – SUGGESTIONS FOR CANADA		
Dress code NAME & Occasion:	**What to wear: Women**	**What to wear: Men**
White tie – VERY formal - some $$$ weddings - galas - state dinners	a formal, floor-length evening gown, usually with formal jewelry & elbow-length gloves. Dressy shoes.	a tail suit (a long black jacket with tails), a white collared shirt, a white vest, a white bow tie, and black patent-leather shoes
Black tie - formal - Evening affairs.	a floor-length evening gown, an elegant knee-length dress or your dressiest black dress. Dressy shoes.	a tuxedo, a black bow tie, a black cummerbund or vest, and black patent-leather shoes
"Creative" Black Tie - formal, but with a trendy twist - **new trend** for weddings & galas	a more fun, but still a formal gown or a formal knee-length dress, a satin ball-gown skirt with a sexy sweater or blouse, or dress pants with a silk top. Dressy shoes.	a tuxedo combined with trendy accessories, such as colourful suspenders, a black shirt or a colourful or patterned bow tie with a matching cummerbund
Semi-formal / Black Tie optional - between formal and casual. Depends on the time of the event. - evening events - concerts - galas	a knee-length cocktail dress, a little black dress, a dressy skirt and top, or even dress pants with a dressy blouse. Dressy shoes or pumps.	a suit and tie in a dark or light colour, depending on the season and the time of day, or dress pants with a collared shirt and jacket. Dress shoes.
Cocktail attire - festive and fun, but not formal - garden weddings - summer parties - cocktail parties - New Year's Eve	a cocktail dress (knee length or as short as you dare!), often quite sexy (low neckline and slit in the skirt). Sexy sandals or heels.	a suit jacket and slacks, with or without a tie. Colours or patterns can be a bit bolder than with semi-formal attire Dress shoes.
Business casual - casual, but work-appropriate - summer parties - conferences - some weddings & funerals	dress pants, a casual dress, or a **skirt with a nice blouse**. Stay away from spaghetti straps or plunging necklines. Pumps or comfortable but not casual shoes (NO runners!)	khakis or dress pants with a collared shirt and loafers (or loafer-style shoes). You can also add a sport coat or blazer.
Casual – everyday wear - friends or family gatherings - BBQs, beach party, picnics - casual weddings	anything goes, including jeans, shorts, and tank tops Runners, sandals or flip-flops. Avoid flip-flops or anything too sexy for bigger events.	T-shirt & jeans; longer shorts; khakis with a golf shirt, a short/long-sleeved shirt or a sweater. Loafers, runners or sandals.

SECRET #34: HOW LONG IS A GET-TOGETHER?

Some POSSIBLE Answers for Canada (with LOTS of individual variations!)

	PARTNER'S Name:	PARTNER'S Name:	
CHALLENGE:	**COUNTRY:**	**COUNTRY:**	**CANADA?**
1. It's normal to start a party in the afternoon and continue for 8+ hours.			Occasionally (family reunions, for example)
2. We will often spend 4+ hours in a restaurant.			Rarely (unless the service is SLOW)
3. Get-togethers at someone's home usually end about midnight.			Yes (May vary by AGE – Younger = LATER)
4. It's common for people to sleep over if the party goes late.			Not usually
5. Children can stay up as late as they want at a get-together (school nights = Sunday-Thursday nights)			No (We expect our kids to go to bed at a reasonable hour if they have to go to school the next day.)
6. Children can stay up as late as they want at a get-together (weekend nights = Fri. & Sat. nights)			Maybe (some families)
7. You can tell your guests directly that they should go home.			Not usually
8. You should **hint** that it's time to go home. (How?)			Yes. Yawning or glancing at your watch or a clock.

Copyright © 2019 Catherine (Kate) Maven PHOTOCOPIABLE BY PURCHASING TEACHER

SECRET #35: COMMON-LAW MARRIAGES
Some POSSIBLE Answers for CANADA:

1. Are couples allowed to live together without a legal marriage? (Live "common law"?)   **Yes**

   - If yes, has this always been true?   **? (I don't know for sure.)**

   - When did it start to change?   **Legal change approved in 1981**

2. Do partners in common-law marriages have the following *same rights and responsibilities* as legally-married partners?

a. Are financially responsible for supporting their biological children (while 'married')?   **Yes**

b. Are financially responsible for supporting their biological children (after separating)?   **Yes**

c. Have the same rights to custody & access to children in the case of a breakup?   **Yes- usually**

d. Have to submit a joint tax return?   **Yes (in Ontario - depends on the Province/Territory)**

e. Can share health benefits offered through work?   **Depends on the company**

f. Have the same access to a partner in the hospital?   **Usually**

g. Have the same right to inherit from their common-law spouse?   **No (unless it's written in your WILL)**

h. Have the same right to 50% of assets in the case of a breakup?   **Usually (in Ontario. Depends on Province / Territory)**

i. Are financially responsible for their common-law spouse's debts?   **Not unless you co-signed**

j. Have the same right to spousal support in the case of a breakup?   **Not usually**

k. Have the same right to welfare and disability benefits   **Yes**

l. Have the same rights regarding immigration sponsorship   **Yes**

m. Have the same right to make health care decisions for their common-law spouse?   **Maybe NOT**

3. Common-law partners can sign an agreement if they want to change some of their rights.
   Yes (same as legally-married couples!)

4.

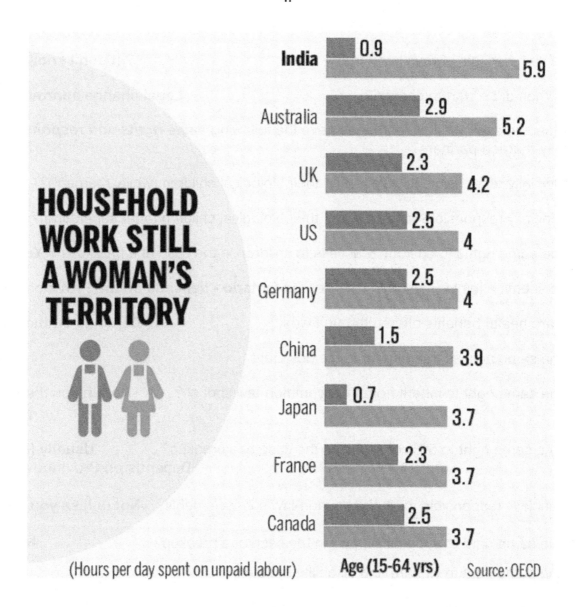

India 0.9 / 5.9
Australia 2.9 / 5.2
UK 2.3 / 4.2
US 2.5 / 4
Germany 2.5 / 4
China 1.5 / 3.9
Japan 0.7 / 3.7
France 2.3 / 3.7
Canada 2.5 / 3.7

HOUSEHOLD WORK STILL A WOMAN'S TERRITORY

(Hours per day spent on unpaid labour)   Age (15-64 yrs)   Source: OECD

(SOURCE: http://indpaedia.com/ind/index.php/Gender_equality:_India)

SECRET #37: KIDS & RESPONSIBILITIES: Age-Appropriate CHORES (SUGGESTIONS)

Chores for children ages 2 to 3
1. Put toys away
2. Fill pet's food dish
3. Put clothes in hamper
4. Wipe up spills
5. Dust
6. Pile books and magazines

Chores for children ages 4 to 5
Any of the above chores, plus:
1. Make their bed
2. Empty wastebaskets
3. Bring in mail or newspaper
4. Clear table
5. Pull weeds, if you have a garden
6. Use hand-held vacuum to pick up crumbs
7. Water flowers
8. Unload utensils from dishwasher
9. Wash plastic dishes at sink
10. Fix bowl of cereal

Chores for children ages 6 to 7
Any of the above chores, plus:
1. Sort laundry
2. Sweep floors
3. Set and clear table
4. Help make and pack lunch
5. Weed garden
6. Rake leaves
7. Tidy bedroom DAILY

Chores for children ages 8 to 9
Any of the above chores, plus:
1. Load dishwasher
2. Put away groceries
3. Vacuum
4. Help make dinner
5. Make own snacks
6. Wash table after meals
7. Put away own laundry
8. Sew buttons
9. Make own breakfast
10. Peel vegetables
11. Cook simple foods, such as toast
12. Mop floor
13. Take pet for a walk

Chores for children ages 10 and older.
Any of the above chores, plus:
1. Unload dishwasher
2. Fold laundry
3. Clean bathroom
4. Wash windows
5. Wash car
6. Cook simple meal with supervision
7. Do own laundry
8. Baby-sit younger siblings (with adult in the home)
9. Clean kitchen
10. Change their bed sheets

SECRET #38: WHAT DO WE DO WITH AGING PARENTS?
POSSIBLE Answers for Canada (with LOTS of individual variations!)

CHALLENGE:	PARTNER'S Name: COUNTRY:	PARTNER'S Name: COUNTRY:	COUNTRY: **CANADA**
1. Parents and even adult children live together all of their lives.			**NO**
2. Parents move in with their oldest son when they can't live independently.			**Maybe**
3. Parents move in with their oldest daughter when they can no longer live independently.			**Maybe**
4. Parents try to live independently until they die.			**YES**
5. Parents go to a government-funded retirement home.			**Maybe**
6. Parents go to a private retirement home, but it doesn't cost a lot.			**NO**
7. Parents go to a private retirement home, and it's VERY expensive.			**Maybe**
8. Other? (Your idea)			

SECRET #39: READING ACTIVITY: EXPLAINING A BLENDED FAMILY: How are they related *NOW?* ANSWERS:

1. Bob is Mary's **first husband (or "ex-husband")** and Mary is Bob's **first wife (or "ex-wife").**

2. Megan and Anna are Bob's **stepdaughters.**

3. Miguel is Claudia's **son** and Bob's **stepson.** (son through remarriage)

4. Bob is Miguel's **stepdad** (dad through remarriage)

5. Miguel is Megan and Anna's **stepbrother** and they are Miguel's **stepsisters** (siblings through marriage)

6. Claudia is Bob's **second wife (or "new wife")** – Even if they are "common-law" (not legally married), we usually refer to them as "husband" and "wife".

7. Claudia is Megan and Anna's **stepmom**, and they are Claudia's **stepdaughters.**

8. Miguel is **not related to** Mary. (But they will probably end up seeing each other at school or family events.)

9. Leon is Mary and Henry's **son.**

10. Leon is Megan and Anna's **half-brother,** and they are Leon's **half-sisters.** (same mother, different father; or same father, different mother).

11. Henry is Mary's **second husband** and Megan and Anna's **stepdad.**

12. They are Henry's **stepdaughters**

13. Leon is **not related to** Bob or Claudia. (But they will probably end up seeing each other at school or family events.)

SECRET #40: LONE-PARENT FAMILIES – ACTIVITY: TRUE OR FALSE?
ANSWERS: (To the best of my knowledge, from information found online)

1. Most lone-parent families are mothers and children. **TRUE**

2. Lone-parent families tend to live in poverty. **FALSE** (for **Women** - about **22%** & for **MEN** – **7%** and both are **DECLINING**)

3. A lone-parent family is a "broken home". May be **TRUE** – children are more likely to suffer from depression and anxiety.

4. Children from a lone-parent family don't do well in school. **TRUE** (but changing)

5. Children from a lone-parent family get in trouble at school. **TRUE** (but changing)

6. Children from a lone-parent family are more likely to join a gang. **FALSE**

(Research contradicts this; lone-parent families have increased steadily, but in general, crime rates have DROPPED in Canada over the past 10 years.)

7. Children from a lone-parent family are more likely to commit a crime. **FALSE** (see #6)

8. Children from a lone-parent family probably graduate from high school. **TRUE** (but fewer than from two-parent families)

9. Children from a lone-parent family probably graduate from university. **FALSE**

10. Children from a lone-parent family go on to become professionals. **FALSE**

11. Children from lone-parent families are more likely to use drugs. **TRUE**

12. Mothers and fathers in lone-parent families are more likely to commit a crime. **FALSE**

13. Mothers and fathers in lone-parent families don't remarry. **FALSE** (76% remarry)

14. If mothers and fathers in lone-parent families do remarry, they will probably end up divorced **TRUE**

15. Mothers and fathers in lone-parent families have less education. Mothers = **TRUE**

16. Mothers and fathers in lone-parent families aren't professionals. **TRUE**

SECRET #43 GETTING ENGAGED
Some *POSSIBLE* answers for CANADA (There is a LOT of individual variation!)

CHALLENGE:	PARTNER'S Name: COUNTRY:	PARTNER'S Name: COUNTRY:	COUNTRY: **CANADA**
1. Marriages are often arranged.			Now = **NO**. (but my French-Canadian grandmother's marriage was arranged)
2. The bride & groom may meet for the first time at their wedding ceremony.			**No**
3. Someone from the bride's or the groom's family may "represent" them. They may not attend their own wedding.			**No**
4. Men and women aren't allowed to go out alone together (date) until they are married. (Need a chaperone)			**No**
5. There is a BIG engagement party.			**Sometimes** (usually associated with wealth)
6. Parents of the groom pay for the engagement party.			Traditionally, parents of the bride paid for it, but today, **cost is usually shared.**
7. When you get engaged, gifts are exchanged between the families of the bride-to-be & the groom-to-be. (How much $$?)			**No** (In some countries, there used to be a "dowry" paid by the groom's father.)
8. Other? (Your idea)			

SECRET #49: CHILD SUPPORT
ANSWERS about CANADA (Ontario)

CHALLENGE:	PARTNER'S Name: COUNTRY:	PARTNER'S Name: COUNTRY:	COUNTRY: **CANADA**
1. Divorce is legal / acceptable.			**Yes**
2. After a divorce, the mother usually gets custody.			**Yes (80% when it's not Joint)**
3. After a divorce, the father usually gets custody.			**Not usually (see above)**
4. After a divorce, the father must pay child support.			**Yes**
5. Child support is mandatory by law.			**Yes**
6. The government sets out the amount of the payment.			**Yes**
7. The wife has to pay taxes on child support payments.			**No**
1. Other? (Your idea)			

SECRET #53: LATERAL THINKING ACTIVITY: SOME POSSIBLE SOLUTIONS!

POSSIBLE SOLUTIONS:

1. Someone got their egg out of the carton in the fridge

2. Someone put an egg (theirs or someone else's) back in the basket

3. There is another basket of eggs beside the first one

4. There is a chicken in the kitchen and someone got an egg from it

5. Someone came in from another room and put an egg in the basket

6. An alien duplicated one person's egg and put the extra one in the basket

7. A geneticist cloned one person's egg and put the extra one in the basket

8. One person had an egg in their pocket and put that one in the basket

9. One person made an egg out of something (clay, Plasticine, blew one out of glass, drew one, knitted one, etc.) and put it in the basket

10. One person is a magician and pulled an egg out of their magic hat

11. The time frame is not given. It might be a week later – this is a new egg

12. None of the eggs are real. They're actually holograms / images in a video game.

13. The egg in the basket is an image that is part of the basket's design

14. One egg slipped and broke when we tried to pick it up, so we left it there

15. The egg in the basket is an optical illusion created by a strong light and an indent in the bottom of the basket.

16. The kitchen is out in the open air, and it's raining eggs.

17. One person MIMED taking an egg, but never actually picked it up.

18. The kitchen is the set in a play, and the acting is so bad that the audience has started to throw eggs, and one landed in the basket.

SECRET #55: COMMUNICATING WITH THE TEACHER
POSSIBLE EMAIL RESPONSES:

#1:   To: awesomeparents@gmail.com
        From: Chris Yu <chrisyu@bestschool.ca>
        Subject: "Me to We" Event - Thur. Nov 12 @ 7 pm

Hi Parents! I just wanted to remind you that we are having our annual "Me to We" event this Thursday. All of the children have prepared skits and songs to show their Best School spirit, and to help raise funds for our charity in Africa. Tickets are $7 per Person, or $15 for a Family Pass. Please RSVP to let me know if you can come, and how many tickets you'd like.

Chris

YOUR RESPONSE: Subject: <u>Olivia Li's family is coming!</u>

Hi Chris, thanks for the reminder! My wife and our other 2 kids are looking forward

to this event – and are happy to support any "Me to We" initiatives.

Please put us down for a Family Pass. We will send the money in Olivia's Agenda tomorrow.

Thanks,
Jeff

***

#2:   To: urkdwazhrt@gmail.com
        From: Chris Yu <chrisyu@bestschool.ca>
        Subject:_bullying incident

Hi Mr. and Mrs. Urkdwazhrt, I'm sorry to tell you that your daughter Janice has been the victim of a bullying incident today. Janice had a book that one of the other girls wanted, and the girl pulled the book roughly out of Janice's hands, causing her to get a small paper cut on her left hand, which required a Band-Aid. The girl apologized, but congruent with our "Zero Tolerance" policy on bullying, she has received a 1-day suspension. Please call me at 905-555-3322 to arrange a time to speak with me about the incident.

Chris

YOUR RESPONSE: Subject: <u>Kids will be kids?</u>

Hi Chris, thanks for letting us know about this incident, even though it was a

minor injury. We think the Zero Tolerance is basically a good idea, but kindergarten kids

DO tussle over toys and books, right? Maybe the apology would have been enough? We

don't think a meeting is necessary at this point, but if there are repeated incidents or a

bigger injury, please let us know.

Thanks,
Peter & Mary Urkdwazhrt
(Janice's parents)

SECRET #56: UNDERSTANDING REPORT CARDS – ANSWERS

1. Most of the time, Akim can successfully make inferences by predicting relevant events when reading non-fiction texts. During class, he was consistently able to predict outcomes by using the title page of Volcanoes of the World and photos in the text Forest Animals. At home, when reading the newspaper, Akim could further build his excellent inferring skills by making predictions from the headlines.

Probable Mark in this Subject? _____**A**_____

2. In Number Sense and Numeration, John needs direct assistance in order to apply the correct operation (e.g. addition or subtraction) when solving problems. He is able to add and subtract 2-digit numbers, using manipulatives and on his whiteboard. However, when solving tasks in his math journal, John consistently needs help to re-examine the problem, highlighting key words to help him choose the correct operation.

Probable Mark in this Subject? _____**D**_____

3. Rebecca is usually able to follow and give basic classroom instructions such as Comment ça va? and Quel temps fait-il? She experienced a bit of difficulty in giving an oral presentation on an assigned topic. Rebecca is encouraged to use available resources and seek feedback from the teacher and her peers. Rebecca can read a simple story and is able to give brief oral responses. In her oral response to the story "Au zoo", Rebecca successfully used pictures to help her with comprehension. She would benefit from an opportunity to read short texts and restate them in her own words. Rebecca is usually able to write simple, short sentences on assigned topics.

Probable Mark in this Subject? _____**B**_____

4. When reading stories with unfamiliar words, Janice is sometimes unable to retell the main ideas from the story due to challenges with reading fluency. With some help, she is able to orally retell ideas from stories (e.g., My Favourite Pet) that use familiar words from the classroom word wall (e.g., dog, cat, fish, home). Janice should practice looking at the whole sentence and reading it out loud to help her guess the meaning of unfamiliar words.

Probable Mark in this Subject? _____**C**_____

SECRET #59: LEARN PHRASAL VERBS WITH 'OFF' – ANSWERS:

1. to fall off (business)	D	1. to criticize someone harshly	
2. to doze off	F	2. "I don't believe you! Are you kidding?"	
3. to go off (alarm)	G	3. to leave suddenly	
4. to tell someone off	A	4. to drop suddenly	
5. to pull off (positive)	i	5. to emit (fumes or gasses)	
6. to come off	J	6. to fall asleep inappropriately	
7. to stay off	H	7. to begin to make loud sounds	
8. to take off	C	8. to not walk or sit on something	
9. to give off	E	9. to succeed (but surprised)	
10. "Come off it!"	B	10. to become detached from something	

DIRECTIONS: Replace the UNDERLINED with the best idiom – ANSWERS:

1. I am sick and tired of my neighbour letting her dog do its business on my lawn. I have asked her nicely. Now I am going to yell at her about it. **(TELL HER OFF)**

2. I don't know what happened to Akim. One minute he was here, and the next, he had left suddenly. **(TAKEN OFF)**

3. Sales of our new produce have dropped suddenly this quarter. **(FALLEN OFF)**

4. It's hard for me to stay awake when I'm studying. I keep falling asleep when I shouldn't. **(DOZING OFF)**

5. "You want me to lend you *more* money? I don't believe you!" **(COME OFF IT!)**

6. We thought the customer hated our presentation, but in the end, we were successful. **(PULLED IT OFF)**

7. "I just washed the kitchen floor. Please avoid walking on it until it dries." **(STAY OFF IT)**

8. It is dangerous to use spray paint without a mask because it emits dangerous fumes. **(GIVE OFF)**

9. About two weeks after I bought my new car, the hub cap separated from the wheel of my car. **(CAME OFF)**

10. I hate my smoke detector sometimes. It rings loudly every time I fry something! **(GOES OFF)**

SECRET #62: DIFFERENCES IN FINDING A JOB
Some POSSIBLE Answers about CANADA:

CHALLENGE:	PARTNER'S Name: COUNTRY:	PARTNER'S Name: COUNTRY:	COUNTRY: **CANADA**
1. You don't need a resume for most jobs.			**No**. While there are places that ask you to fill out an Application Form, MOST companies want a resume.
2. You put your age on your resume.			**No**. It's **ILLEGAL** to ask your age. (Until you're hired. Then it's often on your employment contract!)
3. You put your health condition on your resume.			**No**. It's **ILLEGAL** to ask your health (but employers DO want to know. That's why we put physical activities such as "hiking" & "swimming" on our resumes.
4. You put your marital status on your resume.			**No**. It's **ILLEGAL** to ask your marital status, or whether you have (or want) children.
5. You put your photo on your resume.			**No** (except Actors & Models, and then it's a separate "Head Shot")
6. You use the SAME resume to apply to ALL jobs.			**NEVER**. Each job application should include a resume "tweaked" to focus on the skills for a particular job or company.
7. You must put your legal name on a resume.			**No**. Put whatever name you WANT on a resume. It's essentially a MARKETING DOCUMENT! (Give your legal name once you're HIRED.)
8. Other? (Your idea)			

SECRET #63: THE BENEFITS OF VOLUNTEERING – READING ACTIVITY – ANSWERS:

In addition to providing a valuable reference for future work, research shows that volunteering offers us important psychological and even physical health benefits. For those who suffer from depression, focusing outside of ourselves is a great way to lower our stress and increase feelings of self-worth. It helps us feel connected to our community, and this is especially important when we have moved into a new culture or community. Often, volunteering offers the chance to make new friends, both in clients and co-workers. Volunteering can not only make us happier, it also can add years to our lives, possibly by lowering our stress. There are a number of organizations that will help match you with an appropriate volunteer opportunity. It isn't always working in a hospital! Finally, volunteering will give you a chance to practice your English, learn new hard and soft skills and gain valuable Canadian work experience.

COMPREHENSION QUESTIONS:

1. Name 3 psychological benefits of volunteering that are mentioned in the text *-Here are 4:*

lowers stress   increase self-worth   make friends   feel connected to community

2. How can volunteering help us to live longer?

_____**lowers stress**_____

3. When is volunteering particularly important?

__ when we move into a new culture or community _

4. Name 3 ways that volunteering can help you get a job.

references   new hard & soft skills   Canadian experience

INFERENCES:

5. Why does the text mention that volunteering isn't always in a hospital?

_Many people only associate volunteering with hospitals but there are many other options

6. Why does the author mention self-worth?

_You might be surprised that volunteering increases self-worth.

7. Does this text offer a balanced view of the effects of volunteering?

_No. It focuses only on the positive aspects of volunteering.

SECRET #67: DIVERSITY AT WORK –Some POSSIBLE Answers:

Try to GUESS the answer for each country before you ask! Then survey your classmates, and fill in the following chart: If there is more than one person from a given country, check to see if they agree. If not, list the variations! Which country has the HIGHEST PERCENT OF MINORITIES? Which country has the LOWEST?
NOTE: the United Nations Council on the Elimination of Racial Discrimination has asked Canada to <u>reflect</u> upon its use of the term <u>visible minority</u>

COUNTRY	How many different visible minorities do you have?	Do minorities have EQUAL access to opportunity (like getting HIRED)?	Do visible minorities earn less?	Is racism a problem in this country?
Canada	STATS CANADA says 10 - South Asian, Chinese, Black, Filipino, Latin American, Arab, Southeast Asian, West Asian, Korean and Japanese (more than 7,000,000 people)	No https://globalnews.ca/news/5424465/discriminatory-hiring-practices-canada/	Yes – Men = 18% Women = 3% less	Yes

SECRET #68: IDENTIFYING HARD & SOFT SKILLS
ANSWERS:

accounting	H	adaptability	S	administration	H
analysis	H	attitude	S	automotive	H
banking	H	bookkeeping	H	carpentry	H
communication	S	computer hardware	H	conflict resolution	S
construction	H	creative thinking	S	critical thinking	S
data management	H	decision making	S	design	H
editing	H	electrical	H	engineering	H
financial	H	flexibility	S	healthcare	H
information technology	H	languages	H	legal	H
manufacturing	H	math	H	medical	H
mediation	S	motivation	S	networking	S
nursing	H	pharmaceutical	H	pipefitter	H
plumbing	H	positivity	S	problem-solving	S
programming	H	project management	H	research	H
science	H	software design	H	spreadsheets	H
teaching	H	teamwork	S	telecommunications	H
testing	H	time management	S	translation	H
word processing	H	work ethic	S	writing	H

SECRET #70: WHEN DO WE TELL THE (WHOLE) TRUTH?
Some *POSSIBLE* Answers for CANADA:

CHALLENGE:	PARTNER'S Name: COUNTRY:	PARTNER'S Name: COUNTRY:	COUNTRY: **CANADA**
1. People tell the truth to their parents.			Teens = **NO** Adults = **Usually**
2. People tell the truth to their spouse.			**Usually** (Except "white lies" – lies told in order to be KIND.)
3. People tell the truth to their best friend.			**Usually** (Except "white lies" – lies told in order to be KIND.)
4. People tell the truth to their boss.			**Yes** (Unless they're covering up bad behaviour.)
5. People tell the truth to their clients or customers.			In sales = **NOT always** The rest = Usually
6. People tell the truth to insurance companies.			Often = **NO** (But insurance companies often LIE as well.)
7. People tell the truth to the police.			**Yes** (Unless they're covering up bad behaviour.)
8. People tell the truth to the government.			**Yes** (Unless they're covering up bad behaviour.)
9. People tell the truth to the media.			**Yes** (Unless they're covering up bad behaviour.)
10. Other? (Your idea)			

SECRET #71: WHAT MAKES A GOOD BOSS?
Some *POSSIBLE* Answers for CANADA:

In Canada, we think a Good Boss...

1. Is transparent in communication.

We want a boss that delivers clear expectations of our roles and responsibilities, as well as honest communication about things happening in the company.

2. Gives recognition and praise.

- but BONUSES are also nice!

3. Provides feedback, mentorship, and training.

Because of the importance of Professional Development, it's important to us that our boss is aware of what we need in order to progress in our career, and supports us doing it (financially and time-wise).

4. Creates a feeling of teamwork & community.

Some workplaces foster intense competition between employees as a technique to get everyone to "work harder". Microsoft is famous for this, but it doesn't make for happy employees.

5. "Walks the walk" – not just "talks the talk"

We want a boss who doesn't expect more of you than of him or herself. We want someone who takes action and leads by example.

6. Demonstrates good problem solving.

A *good* boss is someone who doesn't panic when things go wrong. The *best* boss is someone who can DELEGATE appropriately, so that things don't get the CHANCE to go wrong.

7. Avoids micromanaging.

We want our boss to have faith that we can do the job he or she hired us to do. Micromanaging makes us feel mistrusted.

8. Puts people first.

If we feel that our boss values money more than people, we lose loyalty to the company.

SECRET #72: JOB-SEEKING JARGON - MATCHING
ANSWERS:

JOB-SEEKING TERMS		MEANING
1. Background Check	F	a) full-time employment or full-time equivalent
2. Benefits	G	b) job openings that aren't advertised (which is the MAJORITY of job openings in Canada)
3. Corporate Culture	J	c) skills from previous jobs or training which you will be able to easily apply to your next position
4. Curriculum Vitae (CV)	H	d) meeting with a contact to simply learn more about a company or an industry (often leads to a job!)
5. Fit	i	e) individuals/companies that are hired to find qualified candidates for specific positions
6. FTE	A	f) verify the information an applicant provides
7. Hidden Job Market	B	g) from health and dental insurance to paid vacations, sick leave, child care, pension plans, etc.
8. Informational Interview	D	h) similar to a resume; usually used for professions
9. Job Shadowing	K	i) how well a candidate meets the job requirements and how well he/she would mesh with the company culture
10. Keywords	L	j) expectations, values and rules of conduct that are shared and maintained by a company and its employees
11. Recruiters or Headhunters	E	k) spending a short time observing someone while they're working so you can see what's involved
12. Transferable Skills	C	l) terms for which recruiters and HR managers might scan a resume

SECRET #74: WHY DO YOU NEED A MENTOR?
Some *POSSIBLE* Answers:

1) They can give you advice about education or certification

2) They can train you in the "secrets" you need to succeed in your company or industry

3) They can inform you about changes to the industry that may not be generally known

4) They can teach you about Canadian culture

5) They can teach you about corporate culture

6) They can explain the "office politics" in your company

7) They can teach you about networking

8) They often have a Bigger Network, so they can OPEN DOORS

9) They can encourage you when you're not confident

10) They can help you build communication skills

11) They may have already experienced what you're going through

12) They can be a "safe" person to complain to (... but be **CAREFUL**!)

13) They can help you focus on the RIGHT GOAL for your future

14) You can bounce ideas off them before presenting them to a client or team

15) They can be your *friend!*

SECRET #76: K.I.S.S. – KEEP IT SHORT & SIMPLE – WRITING EMAILS
Some POSSIBLE responses:

#1: To: allstaff@awesomestuff.com
From: Chris Yu <hr@awesomestuff.com>
Subject: staff meeting attendance

To all staff – It has come to our attention that many staff members are not attending our quarterly "Where Are We Now?" staff events. Most of the staff members who bother to RSVP have not actually shown up for the actual events! We're hearing what you aren't saying, so now we're asking for your suggestions: What would give you better incentive to attend the next event? (We can't hold it in Florida in February, sorry ... LOL)

Chris

YOUR RESPONSE: Subject: <u>How about holding them during work hours?</u>

Hi Chris, thanks for your reminder about attending WAWN events. Personally,

as a mother of 2 busy pre-teens, I find the timing of these events (5-7 pm) difficult

to manage. It would be better for me if the events could be held during work hours.

Could you please mention this suggestion to management?
Thanks,
Claire

Claire Hudson, M.A.
Head of Customer Satisfaction

***

#2: To: yuyuyu@gmail.com
From: ChrisYu2@gmail.com
Subject:_reschedule dinner?

Hi Yu, I'm really sorry, but we're going to have to reschedule the dinner we'd planned for this coming Saturday night. We were really looking forward to our visit – you're a genius on the BBQ! – but my boss just dumped a TON of work on me and it's going to take all weekend to get it finished. Please also apologize to Patricia and the kids, and maybe your bunch can come over here for dinner in a couple of weeks instead?

Chris

YOUR RESPONSE: Subject: <u>BUMMER! or Sorry to hear that!</u>

Hey Chris, that's too bad! We were really looking forward to seeing you & the fam.

But – hey! – I GET it. Gotta do what we gotta DO. For sure, we'll get together soon. Just

let me know what works for you.
Thanks,
Yu

SECRET #78: STARTING A BUSINESS – INTERNET RESEARCH
Some *POSSIBLE* Answers:

Actually, the **Business Development Bank of Canada** can help answer ALL of these questions, AND connect you to local resources! **https://www.bdc.ca/en/pages/home.aspx**

THING I NEED TO KNOW ABOUT STARTING A BUSINESS IN CANADA	RESOURCE (website or physical address NEAR YOU). Also provide contact phone number, dates & times & any costs, if possible.
1. What kind of business should I start?	https://quickbooks.intuit.com/ca/resources/starting-business/small-business-industry-profitable-canada/
2. Should I buy a franchise?	https://www.theglobeandmail.com/report-on-business/small-business/sb-growth/thirteen-things-to-consider-before-buying-a-franchise-in-canada/article20471510/
3. How do I know if there is a DEMAND for this product or service?	https://www.shopify.ca/blog/13640265-the-16-step-guide-to-evaluating-the-viability-of-any-product-idea
4. Is there a lot of COMPETITION?	https://www.bdc.ca/en/articles-tools/marketing-sales-export/marketing/pages/how-evaluate-competition.aspx
5. Where would I get the money?	https://canadabusiness.ca/starting/financing-your-new-business/
6. How can I find a MENTOR?	https://www.bdc.ca/en/articles-tools/business-strategy-planning/manage-business/pages/how-find-business-mentor-tips-young-entrepreneurs.aspx
7. Should I start an online business or a physical business?	https://canadabusiness.ca/blog/e-commerce-what-to-consider-when-selling-online-in-canada-1/
8. Can someone help me write a BUSINESS PLAN?	https://www.bdc.ca/en/articles-tools/entrepreneur-toolkit/templates-business-guides/pages/business-plan-template.aspx

    PHOTOCOPIABLE BY PURCHASING TEACHER

SECRET #81: EQUAL PAY FOR EQUAL WORK?
Some *POSSIBLE* answers for CANADA:

CHALLENGE:	PARTNER'S Name: COUNTRY:	PARTNER'S Name: COUNTRY:	COUNTRY: CANADA
1. Men earn more than women in general.			**True**
2. Men and women who do the same job earn the same pay.			**By LAW, True. In reality, False.**
3. Men do jobs that women can't do.			**True - to some degree (though this is changing)**
4. "Women's work" – such as childcare – isn't as valuable to the economy.			**This is a PERCEPTION by many people.**
5. Women get promoted as often as men.			**False**
6. There aren't many female CEOs.			**True (<8%)**
7. Women don't want to run companies.			**Maybe True in the past**
8. Women are too emotional to make tough business decisions.			**False**
9. Other? (Your idea)			

SECRET #83: WHAT ARE OUR HUMAN RIGHTS?
The United Nations has issued a UNIVERSAL DECLARATION OF HUMAN RIGHTS.
Here they are (in simple English).

1. We are all born free and equal. We all have our own thoughts and ideas. We should all be treated in the same way.	16. Every adult has the right to marry and have a family if they want to. Men and women have the same rights when they are married, and when they are separated.
2. These rights belong to everybody, whatever our differences.	17. Everyone has the right to own things or share them. Nobody should take our things from us without a good reason.
3. We all have the right to life, and to live in freedom and safety.	18. We all have the right to believe in what we want to believe, to have a religion, or to change it if we wish.
4. Nobody has any right to make us a slave. We cannot make anyone else our slave.	19. We all have the right to make up our own minds, to think what we like, to say what we think, and to share our ideas with other people.
5. Nobody has any right to hurt or torture us or treat us cruelly.	20. We all have the right to meet our friends and to work together in peace to defend our rights. Nobody can make us join a group if we don't want to.
6. Everyone has the right to be protected by the law.	21. We all have the right to take part in the government of our country. Every adult should be allowed to vote to choose their own leaders.
7. The law is the same for everyone. It must treat us all fairly.	22. We all have the right to a home, enough money to live on and medical help if we are ill. Music, art, craft and sport are for everyone to enjoy.
8. We can all ask for the law to help us when we are not treated fairly.	23. Every adult has the right to a job, to a fair wage for their work, and to join a trade union.

… continued …

UNIVERSAL DECLARATION OF HUMAN RIGHTS ... CONTINUED

9. Nobody has the right to put us in prison without a good reason, to keep us there or to send us away from our country.	24. We all have the right to rest from work and to relax.
10. If we are put on trial, this should be in public. The people who try us should not let anyone tell them what to do.	25. We all have the right to enough food, clothing, housing and health care. Mothers and children and people who are old, unemployed or disabled have the right to be cared for.
11. Nobody should be blamed for doing something until it has been proved. When people say we did a bad thing we have the right to show it is not true.	26. We all have the right to education, and to finish primary school, which should be free. We should be able to learn a career, or to make use of all our skills.
12. Nobody should try to harm our good name. Nobody has the right to come into our home, open our letters, or bother us, or our family, without a good reason.	27. We all have the right to our own way of life, and to enjoy the good things that science and learning bring.
13. We all have the right to go where we want to in our own country and to travel abroad as we wish.	28. There must be proper order so we can all enjoy rights and freedoms in our own country and all over the world.
14. If we are frightened of being badly treated in our own country, we all have the right to run away to another country to be safe.	29. We have a duty to other people, and we should protect their rights and freedoms.
15. We all have the right to belong to a country.	30. Nobody can take away these rights and freedoms from us.

SECRET #84: RECOGNIZING ABUSE
Which of the following actions may be considered ABUSIVE (at *HOME* or at *WORK*) in Canada? *ANSWERS:*

1. Throwing something at you such as a phone, book, shoe or plate — **YES**

2. Extramarital affairs — **YES**

3. Humiliating or embarrassing you repeatedly — **YES**

4. Pushing or pulling you — **YES**

5. Isolating you from friends and family — **YES**

6. Grabbing your clothing but not your body — **YES**

7. Controlling the household money alone — **YES (unless you AGREE to this)**

8. Sending you text messages, voicemails, videos, letters, photos and gifts after you have asked them to stop — **YES**

9. Unreasonable jealousy — **YES**

10. Smacking your bottom without your permission or consent — **YES**

11. Forcing you to have sex or perform a sexual act — **YES**

12. Making everything your fault — **YES**

13. Allowing other people (e.g., mother-in-law) to control or yell at you — **YES**

14. Grabbing your face to make you look at them — **YES**

15. Grabbing you to prevent you from leaving or to force you to go somewhere — **YES**

16. Threatening to commit suicide if you leave — **YES**

17. Denying you the right to be alone or spend time with friends and family without your partner — **YES**

18. Constantly calling or texting when you are not with him/her — **YES**

19. Demanding that you share your banking or internet passwords — **YES**

20. Making fun of you — **YES**

21. Yelling at you until you cry — **YES**

22. Threatening you by raising a hand as if to hit you — **YES**

PHOTOCOPIABLE BY PURCHASING TEACHER

SECRET #87: AGE OF MAJORITY
Some answers (for ONTARIO):

CHALLENGE:	PARTNER'S Name: COUNTRY:	PARTNER'S Name: COUNTRY:	COUNTRY: CANADA
1. You are a legal adult at 18 years old.			YES
2. You are a legal adult at 21 years old.			NO
3. You can't own property until you're a legal adult.			YES
4. You can't vote until you're a legal adult.			YES
5. You can drive a car at 16 years old.			YES
6. You can drink alcohol legally at 18.			NO (age 19 in Ontario)
7. You can get married at any age (with parent's permission)			NO (16 with parent's consent; 18 without)
8. You can start working legally at any age.			NO (12 with parent's consent; 15 without)
9. Other? (Your idea)			

SECRET #91: COMPLAINING EFFECTIVELY
ANSWERS:

1. You can't …	D/H	A. … some editing.
2. I wish you wouldn't …	H/D	B. … high taxes.
3. My boss is always griping about …	J	C. … work overtime for no pay.
4. Your report could use … / could do with …	A	D. … eat that entire pizza yourself!
5. I wish my students would …	i	E. … this shoddy workmanship.
6. The citizens are protesting …	B	F. … bark all night.
7. I refuse to …	C	G. … the poor service you've given us.
8. Our customers won't accept …	E	H. … smoke on your balcony. The smoke always blows in my windows.
9. Her dog tends to …	F	I. … complete their homework all the time.
10. I'd like to speak to your manager about …	G	J. … paying us overtime.

How do you complain in the following situations? Some POSSIBLE ANSWERS:

PROBLEM	COMPLAINT or REQUEST
My office is cold.	Could you please turn up the heat?
My pay is wrong.	Hi, I think there's a mistake on my pay. Could you please check it out? Thanks!
My co-worker keeps making sexist remarks.	I have asked you before not to say such sexist things to me. If you continue to say stuff like this, I'm going to report you to Human Resources.
My co-worker keeps making racist remarks.	I have asked you before not to say such racist things to me. If you continue to say stuff like this, I'm going to report you to Human Resources.
The fridge at work is always stinky.	Send a MEMO: Attention All Staff: It has come to our attention that someone is leaving food in the fridge WAY past its Expiry Date. As of the 1st of next month, any food remaining in the fridge on Friday afternoons will be put in the garbage.

… continued …

SECRET #91: COMPLAINING EFFECTIVELY
ANSWERS – CONTINUED

PROBLEM	COMPLAINT or REQUEST
My co-worker has bad breath or B.O. (Body Odor).	Hi, Henry. Can I speak privately to you for a moment? I don't know a nice way of saying this, but you always seem to have bad breath/B.O. I just thought I'd tell you because if it was me, I'd want to know.
The clients keep calling ME, when they should be speaking to my team leader.	Hello, Mr. Smith. Yes, I understand that you have questions/concerns, but unfortunately, I am not in a position to help you. As I told you several times in the past, it would be best for you if you would speak to my Team Leader, Ms. Maven.
I have a designated parking space, but somebody else keeps parking there.	Hi, Margaret, I'm not sure if you're aware, but we each have a designated parking spot and you've been parking in mine … Could you please check with H.R. or Security and find out where you should be parking?
My co-worker keeps criticizing my work even though he's my equal.	Hi, Mark. Can I have a word with you? I guess you know that English isn't my first language, and I appreciate your help in improving my emails, but it's really embarrassing for me when you criticize me in front of the rest of the team. I would appreciate it if, in future, you would tell me privately, either in person or on the phone, if you think I've made a mistake.
Someone always smokes just outside the door that I use to enter the building.	Hi, Mary. I am just wondering if you're aware of the company policy that no one is supposed to smoke within 5 metres of any door to the building. The reason I'm mentioning it is because I have asthma and inhaling cigarette smoke makes it much worse.
My neighbour's children are always riding their bikes in my driveway.	(Say nothing if you want to stay friends with the children's parents.) or … Hi, Peter … I'm not sure if you're aware of this, but your kids are always riding their bikes in my driveway, and I'm really afraid I'm going to run into one of them some day when I'm backing out of my garage. I think it's a real safety hazard, so could you please ask them not to ride in my driveway in the future?

SECRET #92: The BAD NEWS SANDWICH – REWRITING EMAILS
POSSIBLE SOLUTIONS:

#1. **To:** badbob@ABCbank.ca
From: supervisor@ABCbank.ca
Subject: Tardiness

Bob, you have arrived late 3 times this month. If you don't shape up, you're going to get FIRED.
U.R. Intrable, Manager

Your REWRITE:

Dear Bob, you have been a diligent and accurate bank teller with ABC bank for the past three

years, and we appreciate your contribution to the bank's success.

However, it has been noted that you have arrived late 3 times this month. As you know, the bank

has strong expectations for punctuality, and your supervisor, Janet Abrams, has stated that she

has mentioned this issue to you and said you promised to improve. If you are having personal

issues which affect your ability to arrive on time, please contact HR and let them know, and we

will try to be as accommodating as possible. Thank you for your attention to this matter.
U.R. Intrable, Manager

#2. **To:** badparents@gmail.com
From: goodteacher@bestschool.ca
Subject: Erica's failing

Dear Mr. and Mrs. Badparents,
This is to inform you that your daughter Eric is failing Grade 1 and will probably have to repeat her year.
Ms. Goodteacher

Your REWRITE:

Dear Mr. and Mrs. Badparents, we are writing to let you know about a concern we have

regarding the academic performance of your daughter Erica, in Grade 1. While Erica did very well

in Kindergarten last year, and Grade 1 is always a time of change and adaptation, we're afraid

that Erica is falling significantly behind the performance of her classmates.

We are recommending that Erica be tested for a learning disabilities, as well as be given a psychological

assessment. We think it is crucial to find out, sooner rather than later, if Erica has issues which are

affecting her success in school. As per Board Policy, once we determine the cause of Erica's delays,

we will meet with you to discuss an Individual Education Plan (IEP) for her.

If you would like to meet sooner to discuss how best to support Erica's education, we would be happy to
get together at a mutually convenient time.

Kind regards,
Ms. Goodteacher

SECRET #95: THINKING ABOUT SEXISM
ANSWERS:

What are the major warning signs for a heart attack in MEN?

1. Chest pain

2. Pressure, tightness, pain, or a squeezing or aching sensation in your chest or arms that may spread to your neck, jaw or back.

3. Nausea, indigestion, heartburn or abdominal pain

4. Shortness of breath

5. Fatigue

6. Lightheadedness or sudden dizziness

What are the major warning signs for a heart attack in WOMEN?

1. *May NOT have chest pain!*

2. Nausea or lightheadedness

3. Fatigue (My 59-year-old mother said this about her heart attack: "I had no strength in my legs. I couldn't stand up.")

4. Uncomfortable pressure, squeezing, fullness or pain in the center of your chest

5. Pain or discomfort in one or both arms, the back, neck, jaw or stomach

6. Shortness of breath with or without chest discomfort

7. Cold sweat

SECRET #97: MONEY OR RESPECT?
Some POSSIBLE ANSWERS (2019) for Canada.

	TOP 10 *BEST PAID* JOBS CANADA (STATS Canada – 2019)
1.	Federal judges -$308,600- $396,700
2.	Specialist physicians – $117,00-$375,000
3.	Family physicians – $58,015 – $310,054
4.	Dentist – $53,805 – $213,671
5.	Chief Executive Officer (CEO) – $146,912
6.	Lawyers – $48,630 – $146,431
7.	Senior managers (not Finance or Communications) – $75,159 – $141,569
8.	Senior managers in Finance and Communications – $77,805 – $129,629
9.	Engineering managers – $68,100-$172,000
10.	Actuaries – $45,820 – $129,740
	TOP 10 *MOST RESPECTED* JOBS in Canada 2019 SURVEY:
1.	Nurses
2.	Farmers
3.	Veterinarians
4.	Scientists
5.	Doctors
6.	Teachers
7.	Architects
8.	Engineers
9.	Accountants
10.	Dentists
11.	*EXTRA: Police Officers*

Made in the USA
Monee, IL
24 February 2021